STRATEGIC PRICING FOR THE ARTS

With roughly half of all income for nonprofit arts organizations in the United States coming from earned revenue rather than donations and state funding, the issue of pricing is paramount to success in the arts industry, yet pricing is not covered in any existing textbooks. How should prices differ between ordinary and premium seating? How much of a discount in admission charges should be offered through membership or season subscription? When does it make sense to partner with organizations to offer discounts?

Arts managers, whether working in the performing arts, museums, or festivals, and whether in the commercial, nonprofit, or state sector, need to make informed decisions on the prices they set. This accessible text provides the first concise, practical, non-technical guide for setting prices in the arts industry.

Offering a practical introduction to pricing, this book is perfectly suited to students studying arts management/administration as well as new managers working in the creative and cultural industries.

Michael Rushton is Professor and Director of Arts Administration Programs at Indiana University, USA.

This book is essential reading for anyone involved with Arts Management. Michael Rushton provides the first comprehensive guide to setting prices in the Arts markets – a toolkit of advice in understanding how to determine ticket prices, discounts, and concessions.

Rachel Pownall, *Associate Professor, Tilburg University, the Netherlands*

With declining subscription rates and the growth of dynamic pricing in ticket sales, arts organizations' leaders urgently need a clear and systematic approach to the art of price-setting. Rushton's strategic guide is a superb and indispensable resource.

Patricia Dewey, *Associate Professor and Director, Arts and Administration Program, University of Oregon, USA*

This comprehensive yet straightforward portrayal of options for maximizing revenue will allay any skeptic's concerns that strategic pricing is elitist or a threat to accessibility and patron relations. Implementing effective pricing techniques will increase engagement, participation and revenue. It is a practice long overdue across the arts sector.

Dan J. Martin, *Professor, Carnegie Mellon University, USA*

STRATEGIC PRICING FOR THE ARTS

Michael Rushton

LONDON AND NEW YORK

First published 2015
by Routledge
2 Park Square, Milton Park, Abingdon, Oxon OX14 4RN

and by Routledge
711 Third Avenue, New York, NY 10017

Routledge is an imprint of the Taylor & Francis Group, an informa business

British Library Cataloguing in Publication Data
A catalogue record for this book is available from the British Library

Library of Congress Cataloging in Publication Data
Rushton, Michael, 1959–
Strategic pricing for the arts / Michael Rushton.—First [edition].
pages cm
Includes bibliographical references and index.
1. Arts—Marketing. 2. Pricing. I. Title.
NX634.R87 2014
700.68′1—dc23
2014002023

ISBN: 978-0-415-71366-5 (hbk)
ISBN: 978-0-415-71367-2 (pbk)
ISBN: 978-1-315-88314-4 (ebk)

Typeset in Bembo
by Book Now Ltd, London

Printed and bound in Great Britain by
TJ International Ltd, Padstow, Cornwall

CONTENTS

ILLUSTRATIONS

Figures

Tables

ACKNOWLEDGMENTS

I wish to give thanks to family and friends who have given such support and encouragement in the writing of this book. I also thank the arts managers in the field who were generous with their time in discussing how they go about setting prices in their organizations. I am grateful to Douglas McLennan for giving me the chance to air ideas and opinions on arts pricing through my blog, hosted by his invaluable website ArtsJournal.com. My thanks also go to Terry Clague and Sinead Waldron at Routledge for their assistance and patience as I prepared the manuscript, and on the editorial side to Richard Cook and Andrea Platts for making this short book a much better read. Thanks also to Ashley Dillon for preparing the figures.

At Indiana University, I have had the good fortune to teach outstanding future arts leaders in our program in Arts Administration, and I am thankful to have had the chance to engage with them on the topics covered in this book, especially so for those who said, in the end, "this subject was a lot more interesting than I thought it would be!" Also at IU, I cannot thank enough Megan Starnes, whose tireless work for the Arts Administration program allowed me the opportunity to write this book.

1

INTRODUCTION

Arts organizations need revenue. Museums, performing arts organizations, and festivals need funds to be able to meet their expenses. These funds can come from grants from public sector arts councils or private foundations, from donations by individuals and businesses, from the sale of advertising, or from corporate sponsorships. This book is about one source of revenue in particular: prices charged to members of the audience. The goal is to give arts managers tools they can apply in setting prices strategically, and in so doing further the goals of their organization more effectively, whether it is in the commercial, nonprofit, or public sector. Students of arts management should find this a useful introduction to a topic of very practical import in their future careers. Those already working in the field will hopefully gain some new perspectives on price-setting. Although this is a book about pricing in the arts, it draws freely from other fields – news media, restaurants, hotels, airlines, clothing, and electronics, for example – that provide relevant insights for the cultural sector.

The approach in this book is to provide a systematic way of thinking about pricing in all its aspects. It is not written as a "cookbook," with a set of recipes for dealing with different pricing issues, but rather it is designed to give the reader a method for thinking strategically about pricing. It will show that a common framework can be used to deal with such seemingly disparate questions as: How much of a discount ought to be given to students? Is it better to have a low admission fee with additional charges for exhibitions within the venue, or a higher admission fee with everything free once inside? How does one choose a partner organization with which to offer a joint discount?

How much should a subscription cost relative to the cost of a single show? Of course, practicing arts managers have faced the task of having to answer these questions, and might finish this book by thinking, "well, that's just common sense!" But even in that case, if the book provides confirmation of why their successful practices have been common sense, there is a value in that. If we were to visit a local billiard parlor, it would likely (although not certainly) be the case that the best player would not be able to explain the laws of physics that governed the choice and technique of each shot; the player simply "knows" what to do. Here is hoping that even a very successful manager, like a very successful billiard player, can learn something from a systematic analysis of the decisions they make.

There is a deep, and lively, research literature on pricing strategy. But it is, for the most part, inaccessible to those lacking a post-graduate degree in economics, being highly mathematical, and relying upon a comprehensive understanding of microeconomic theory. In the pages that follow I will draw upon the insights from this body of research, but I will present it without presuming any background knowledge of theory or advanced mathematical techniques. As this is meant to be a practical guide, the text will not be laden with footnotes, although I will conclude each chapter with a list of sources.

Are there not software programs that can solve the pricing problem for you? Indeed, on the market there are programs and services that can track ticket sales of all types for past and current events, and these are very helpful to managers in understanding the patterns of customer demand. As we will see, knowing these patterns will be very helpful in making decisions on prices. But although the software programs provide useful information, they will not tell you what prices to charge. Price-setting remains an art, and this book is meant to develop your skills in that art.

Strategic pricing begins with one single insight: the customers to whom you might sell a ticket to your event differ in the maximum amount they would be willing to pay. To illustrate, consider the following example. Figure 1.1 presents the *demand curve* for tickets for an outdoor performance by a touring symphony orchestra, on a Saturday afternoon in June. There is to be only one performance, and all tickets are for general admission. The demand curve presents the organizer's best estimate, based on past experience of similar events, for the expected number of tickets that would be sold at various prices. At a price of $30, we expect 300 tickets to sell, at a price of $20, we expect 400 tickets to sell, and at a price of $18, we expect demand to be 420 tickets. At a price of just $5, demand would be 550 tickets, and if the event were free, with a price of $0, 600 people would attend. Although

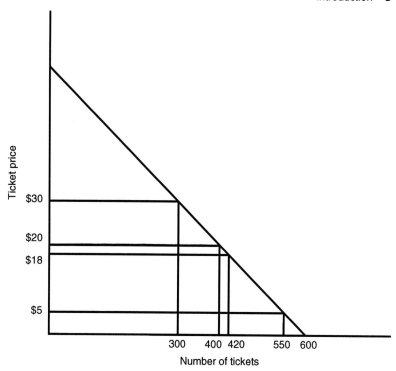

FIGURE 1.1 Demand curve for a symphony concert

in this example the demand curve appears as a straight line, in other cases it might be curved; it depends on this particular market. In every case, however, we expect it to be downward sloping: the higher the price, the fewer tickets we will sell, an expectation that economists have elevated to the status of the *law of demand*.

Following Chapter 2, in which we introduce some useful terms and concepts, in Chapter 3 we consider the case of the organizer for this performance who has just one price to choose: general admission. We will derive a rule for setting this single price in a way that maximizes the profits (revenues minus costs) from the event. This rule will be important as we proceed to more complex pricing problems.

Note something about the demand curve from Figure 1.1. According to the figure, there are 300 people who are willing to pay at least $30 to attend the performance. There are another 100 people who are willing to pay at least $20, but not as much as $30, for the event. The term we will use to denote the maximum that an individual would be willing to pay for admission is *reservation price.* There are 20 people whose reservation price is something between $18 and $20. And there are 50 people whose reservation price is between $0 and $5. If this event involves just a single, general admission price, then those with a reservation price at that amount or higher will attend, and those with a reservation price lower than the announced price will not attend.

The essence of strategic pricing is the recognition that different members of your potential audience have different reservation prices, and that you can increase net profits by segmenting your audience according to what they are willing to pay, charging a higher price to those with higher reservation prices, and a lower price to those with lower reservation prices. Economists refer to this kind of audience segmentation as *price discrimination*, which is perhaps unfortunate, as the word "discrimination" can carry negative undertones, and hints at the notion that it works to the disadvantage of consumers. But it will be shown that some consumers can benefit from the practice. Chapters 4 through 8 explore various, and not mutually exclusive, means of price discrimination.

Chapter 4 considers what is known as *direct price discrimination*, where the audience is segmented into easily identified and verifiable groups, to whom different prices are charged. A common example of this is concessionary admission fees for students, seniors, or the unemployed. Arts presenters can take what knowledge they have of the patterns of reservation prices within each group and set differential prices.

Chapters 5 through 8 involve *indirect price discrimination*. In this case, we know something about patterns of reservation prices, but not enough to allow potential customers to be sorted into identifiable groups. With indirect price discrimination, each potential customer is offered a range of options – a menu – from which to choose. Audience members effectively sort themselves according to their reservation prices.

The first application of indirect price discrimination, presented in Chapter 5, is *two-part pricing*. To take a canonical example, suppose you are setting prices for an amusement park and must choose, first, an admission fee, and, second, a price for each ride within the park. Other things being equal, the higher the price per ride, the lower the amount a customer would be willing to pay as an admission fee. What is the best combination of admission fee and price per ride? It turns out that the best combination depends upon what we think we know about the different preferences embodied in those with high and low reservation prices. More specifically, we can imagine that some visitors simply enjoy the experience of visiting the amusement park, but will only be interested in taking part in a few rides. Other visitors are there only for the rides, it is their primary motivation for attending. If we learn that high reservation price visitors tend to fall into one of these two categories, that information can be exploited in the choice of how to balance admission fees and ride prices. The chapter will consider applications of this technique in the arts.

Chapter 6 will examine pricing when the presenter is able to offer varying quality of experience. Performing arts venues set different prices for different seats or for different performance times; publishers set different prices for hard covers, paperbacks, and e-books; record companies produce ordinary and deluxe versions of CDs. It is no surprise that lower quality versions sell for lower prices. But how big should the price differential be? And what choices are involved in creating the quality differentials in the first place?

In Chapter 7 we consider pricing over varying quantities of offerings. Examples include subscription series and memberships, and we will consider how to set price differentials between single and multiple visits, or even whether customers ought to have a choice at all. Consider that my cable television provider does not allow me to purchase just one channel to view, but instead I must purchase a bundle of channels. Why do they insist upon this, and what can arts managers learn from the example?

Chapter 8 looks at the practice of *tied sales*, where customers receive a discount if they purchase different goods as a package. Theatre patrons in London are offered deals that combine a pair of tickets with a dinner from a (limited) choice of restaurants. What are the advantages to the theatre company in making such an offer? If the motive is to make attending the theatre more attractive, why not simply lower the price of tickets? We will look at cases where tied sales make sense, and how best to choose the package of offerings.

Again, we will see that two-part pricing, quality differentials, bundles, and tied sales are all means of separating those potential customers with high reservation prices from the rest, and finding ways to draw more revenue from those customers than it is possible to obtain from those with lower reservation prices. I will note at the outset that segmenting customers by their willingness to pay is not a way of deceiving patrons, or of tricking them, or of exploiting patterns of irrationality. While these practices are not unheard of within the economy, the strategic pricing techniques covered in this book are respectful of the intelligence of the arts consumer and advocate transparency in what is put before them.

Chapter 9 covers the topic of changing the price of a specific event over time, whether the change is announced to patrons well in advance (for example, when it is made clear that tickets purchased on the day of the event will cost more), or when the change, if any, is not predictable, and is based upon the revealed demand for tickets after they have gone on sale; this is the practice known as *dynamic pricing*. Dynamic pricing is familiar to us from the hotel and airline sectors, but has recently come to be used in some arts and professional sports organizations. In this chapter the technique for applying dynamic pricing will be explained, along with its pitfalls; it remains unclear whether the practice will become widely adopted.

Finally, Chapter 10 looks at pricing when social mission would dictate a departure from profit-maximizing strategies. Many readers of this book will either be working or intend to work in the nonprofit or public sector. I placed this topic at the end of the book because I believe it is important for arts managers in organizations with a nonprofit mission to understand the techniques of strategic pricing first. Only then is it possible to systematically consider departures from these rules in order to further the mission of the organization. It is common for nonprofit arts organizations to employ all of the techniques of strategic pricing covered in this book, and a better understanding of pricing methods can assist nonprofit arts managers in determining the situations where price adjustments are warranted.

I have taught students the analysis presented in this book for a number of years now. The students in our program typically arrive with a background in music or theatre or visual arts, but rarely in economics or business. And it is remarkable how many of these students have said to me afterwards, "I expected this subject to be really boring, but it's actually quite interesting!" I hope so. Learning to understand pricing will not only make you a more effective arts manager, but also give you insights into the various goods and services you buy for your household, such as groceries, or electronics, or vacation packages. At the very least, when a friend tells you about the pricing policies of some store and asks aloud, "Now why exactly would they do that?" you can surprise them with an answer.

Sources

The analogy of the billiard player is from Friedman (1953). A recent excellent, but very mathematically sophisticated, text on pricing is Shy (2008). Other surveys of strategic pricing, also forbidding to those without advanced training in mathematical economics, but from which I will draw some of the ideas presented in this book, are Tirole (1988) and Varian (1989). Less theoretical, but rigorous and with a dose of humor, is McAfee (2002).

2

PRELIMINARIES

This chapter introduces the key terms and the framework for analysis that will be applied throughout the rest of the book to our central problem of how to set prices. The key principle I want to introduce is that of considering marginal benefits and marginal costs in making decisions. I will illustrate this principle with a variety of scenarios to show the general applicability of the method across the spectrum of management problems, and we will then apply the method to pricing in all the chapters that follow.

Here is our first case: I teach at a university with a very distinguished school of music, full of dedicated students. Consider one student, Maggie, who is studying for a degree in piano performance. Outside of her lessons with her principal instructor, she has been practicing piano 25 hours per week. Should Maggie increase the number of hours to 26?

First, we need to know the marginal benefit of increasing the number of hours spent practicing. *Marginal benefit* is defined as the gains realized from increasing any activity by a small amount. In Maggie's case, we need to know the gain from that additional hour; we don't need to know the total value of her attending university or choosing to study music performance, we just need to know how much she would gain from *that hour*. The gains would come in various forms: she might feel greater personal satisfaction as her abilities improve; she might feel good about the increased respect she would receive from her teachers and peers; and she might see the extra practice as something that increases the number of opportunities for future performances. No two people are alike, and so there is no formula to which we can turn. But Maggie will have a sense of what the marginal benefits are to her, which is what matters.

We have been asking about the marginal benefit to Maggie from increasing the number of hours per week she practices from 25 to 26. But if she did adopt a new schedule of practicing 26 hours per week, we could then ask about the marginal benefit of a twenty-seventh hour per week, and a twenty-eighth, and so on. In general, we expect that for most things we do there are *diminishing marginal benefits* the more time we devote to any activity. If Maggie were to keep increasing the amount she practices each week, the gains she would receive from an *additional* hour would gradually fall; the extra practice time would have less and less impact on the quality of her performance. The notion of diminishing marginal benefits applies generally to how we spend our time, whether in things we do for pleasure or things we do in work. The hours I devote to preparing for the lectures I give at my university improve the quality of the classes, but for each additional hour per week I devote to class preparation there is a smaller and smaller gain from allocating one more hour to the task. I enjoy gardening, but there are diminishing marginal benefits to the hours I will devote to it on a typical April weekend; each additional hour yields less return in terms of the beauty of the garden, and of my own pleasure in getting my hands dirty.

The second thing we need to know in solving Maggie's problem is the marginal cost of an hour of practice. *Marginal cost* is defined as the cost of increasing any activity by a small amount. For Maggie, this cost would be all about her time. All of us share the problem of there being only 168 hours in a week, which we need to allocate across work, study, household duties, time spent with family, friends, or alone, and, of course, sleep. The more time we devote to any one activity necessarily means less time for some other valuable activity. Were Maggie to increase her hours per week at the piano from 25 to 26, it would mean less time for studying her other courses, or at her part-time job (which means a cost in the form of reduced earnings), or simply time to relax on her own. Note what is *not* included in marginal cost: I have not included the tuition fees she pays to the university for taking this degree, or what she has paid for her instrument (if she owns one), or the cost of the scores of the pieces she is trying to learn. Those are costs that do not vary whether she practices 25 hours per week or 26, and so are not a part of marginal cost. It is not that tuition fees do not matter – they are a genuine and significant cost to Maggie in attending university, and would have mattered greatly in the decision of whether to pursue her degree. But tuition fees are not a part of the marginal cost of practice time.

Just as Maggie experiences diminishing marginal benefits to her hours of practice, so she will also experience *increasing marginal costs*. The more hours per week she devotes to practice, the fewer she has left for everything else, and it becomes increasingly costly to give up another hour of free time to devote to the piano. If she were only practicing a few hours each week, she might find she had lots of unoccupied time on her hands, and the marginal cost of an hour of practice would be low. But eventually, as she practices more each week and finds herself increasingly pressed for time, the marginal costs of practice will rise.

And now we are ready to answer the question we set at the beginning of this chapter: should Maggie increase the number of hours she practices each week from 25 to 26? If the marginal benefit of doing so exceeds the marginal cost, the answer is "yes." If the gains from an additional hour of practice exceed the costs of that additional hour, it is worth doing. If that seems obvious – of course we will do something if the benefits exceed the costs! – note the importance of the term "marginal." Sound decision-making requires being able to identify and isolate the *marginal* benefits and costs. Maggie's decision on practice hours is independent of tuition fees, apartment rental, and the cost of music books.

What then represents the *best* number of hours for Maggie to practice each week? Suppose that, in fact, it were the case that at 25 hours per week the marginal benefits of practice exceeded the marginal cost, and she followed our suggested rule and began increasing the amount of practice time. As she does this, we expect two things to happen: the marginal benefits of practice will be diminishing, the more hours she devotes to practice, and the marginal costs will be rising, as her time for other activities grows increasingly scarce. Eventually, at a certain number of hours per week, marginal benefits will have fallen and marginal costs will have risen such that they become equal. And that is where we find the best number of hours for her to practice. We should increase any activity so long as marginal benefits exceed marginal costs, but should settle on the amount where marginal benefits equal marginal costs. Were we to pursue the activity beyond this point, the additional amounts of the activity would carry a cost that exceeds the marginal benefits, which would be making us worse off. If we find ourselves pursuing some activity where marginal costs exceed marginal benefits, we should *reduce* the amount until we find the point where marginal benefits and costs are equal. *The optimal amount of any activity is where marginal benefits equal marginal costs.*

This rule for decision-making – increase any activity so long as marginal benefits exceed marginal costs, and settle at the level where marginal benefits equal marginal costs – is the fundamental rule that will guide making choices in price-setting, and in all other management decisions. It is the key to thinking strategically. For any possible course of action, you will be asking yourself what are the *additional* benefits this will bring and what are the *additional* costs. One of the most common errors in decision-making is to lose sight of this by paying undue attention to expenses which are not marginal to the issue at hand, but which are *sunk costs*: costs which must be covered regardless of the decision you are facing. Maggie's tuition fees for attending university are a sunk cost when it comes to the decision of how many hours to practice each week – she owes that money regardless of her practice time. True, they are a *large* cost, and were relevant to the decision to attend university (on *that* decision tuition fees were indeed a marginal cost), but they are not relevant to the hours-of-practice decision.

Notice that orienting your thinking in terms of marginal benefits and marginal costs does *not* mean that everything is being reduced to monetary values. The marginal benefits to Maggie from increasing weekly practice time are complex, and depend to a large degree on the personal satisfaction she gains from developing her artistry. Likewise, the marginal costs of extra practice, which are centered around a problem we all face – the scarcity of time – are concerned with how her hours in other pursuits, not just paying ones, will be affected.

There has been much discussion in recent times on the "economic value of the arts," with concerns that this value is coming to trump all others in considerations of cultural policy. But adopting the marginal-benefit/marginal-cost rule for making decisions is *not* a move to stress the monetary value of the arts above all other benefits, and it applies, as we will see, to nonprofit and public sector organizations just as much as it does to commercial ones. Non-monetary benefits are certainly hard to measure, and are subject to disagreement. But the principle of comparing marginal benefits to marginal costs holds, even in cases where those benefits are complex and hard to articulate.

Consider the following example from the public sector: when is it a good policy to increase the amount of public art in a city, and when would you know you had the "right" amount? When it comes to public projects, the marginal costs are usually straightforward, and monetary: the expenses involved in paying the artist to create the new work, the cost of the space it will occupy, and the future costs of maintenance. But the marginal benefits are more difficult to find: since all members of the community will have some chance to enjoy the art, we need to sum the benefits to all of them, even though those benefits will vary between individuals. The marginal benefits will typically depend on how much art is already in place; there are diminishing marginal benefits for public amenities just as there are for things we enjoy privately. Since this will be very hard to calculate, in the end the choice will come down to political judgment (note there are methods, known as contingent valuation, whereby the researcher asks a sample of individuals what they would be willing to pay in order to increase, or preserve, a public amenity, but such methods are imprecise and remain the subject of controversy: see the sources at the end of this chapter). Having said that, the principle of looking to the margin in making the decision holds. The key is not to try to solve the problem of the value of public art as a whole, but instead to focus on how much the public would gain from an *increase* in the amount of public art, given what is already there.

Let us consider some other applications of this rule. Suppose your theatre company has been having a successful run of a show, better in fact than had been predicted. Should you add a few more performances? The way to think about this systematically would be to consider the marginal benefits and marginal costs. Marginal benefits would consist of the increase in revenues arising from the extra performances (this would have to be calculated net of any audience members purchasing a ticket to one of the added shows as a substitute for an available ticket to a performance from the initially scheduled run), plus any increase in public goodwill towards the theatre for responding to customer demand. Marginal costs involve any additional expenses from the added performances, but must *only* consider the *additional* expenses: the time of the performers, crew and management devoted to the additional performances, additional marketing expenses, and the cost of the performance space for the extra few days, but *not* the costs of rehearsal, design, the initial marketing campaign, or any other costs that were sunk into the initially scheduled run. Extra performances should be added only if the marginal benefits of those performances exceed their marginal cost. Marginal benefits will be declining with the number of performances; each additional performance will be expected to yield a smaller and smaller amount of additional revenue and goodwill. Eventually a point is reached where marginal benefit just equals marginal cost, and that ought to be the final performance.

Note that the rule of looking to the margin on the question of whether to extend the run applies even if the run of the show, as a whole, has turned out to be regrettable. Suppose that mounting the play that we have been discussing had significant and unexpected costs. For example, suppose the deal with the firm that was to rent the sets for the show fell through at the last minute, causing you to have to construct an alternative that proved much more costly, so much so that had you known that cost in advance you would not have produced this work. But that is a sunk cost when it comes to the question of adding performances; the unexpected, and expensive, construction is a cost whether you increase the number of performances or not, and it does not play a role in the decision. Suppose a colleague says "Well, if we add some performances, we can spread the cost of the construction over a greater number of shows, lowering the cost." A response would be, "The cost of the set is fixed regardless of the number of times we use it; if the additional revenues from added performances do not cover additional costs, then the added performances are not worth doing." Sunk costs are, well, sunk.

Richard Caves applied this reasoning to the question of why some big-budget Hollywood films are released to cinemas even when, at the time of release, all indications are that the film was a costly mistake, over which the studio will lose tens of millions of dollars. If, once the film is made, the studio knows (or at least has a pretty strong intuition) that the movie will in the end be a big money loser, why release it? The answer is that the studio will, rationally, look to the marginal benefits and marginal costs of release. Before a movie has been shown, its revenues to that point will have been zero, but there will have been a lot of costs, which are now sunk. So long as the expected revenue from releasing the movie covers the *remaining* (i.e. marginal) costs – these would be the costs of marketing and distribution – then it is worth releasing. If a movie cost $100 million to make, and marketing and distribution would cost $50 million, then as long as expected revenues (including foreign distribution, DVDs, television rights and so on) exceed $50 million, the movie is worth releasing, even though it would take revenues of at least $150 million for the film to have ultimately been a wise investment.

Now consider another application. Suppose you are considering adding an employee to the marketing department of your organization. The marginal benefits in this case are the degree to which the mission of the firm, whether for-profit or nonprofit, will be further enhanced by this additional employee. Marginal benefits will be declining with the number of employees; each additional employee contributes a smaller amount at the margin than the one before. The marginal costs are the wages and benefits needed to compensate the employee, plus any additional capital and materials expenditures that need be made to allow the employee to do his or her work. We hire more people according to whether their marginal benefit exceeds their marginal cost, and will have the optimal number of staff when the marginal benefit has fallen to where it is just equal to marginal cost.

Consumers also apply the rules of marginal benefits and marginal costs (even if they are not themselves aware of these terms).

First, think about the familiar consumer problem of wanting to buy an item, and searching for the best combination of quality and price. We address this issue in small purchases, such as wanting to buy a bottle of water, and in making very significant purchase decisions like buying a car or a house. We know that different sellers have different prices and qualities on offer. At any given moment, buyers have the option of either purchasing the best deal they have seen up to that point, or continuing the search in the hope of finding a better offer. How does the buyer decide?

The marginal costs of prolonging the search would consist of all the additional costs in time and transportation of continuing to shop around, plus the costs of delaying acquiring the item. The marginal benefits of continuing the search are given by the product of (1) the probability that the buyer will actually find a better deal, and (2) the expected value of that better deal relative to the best offer that has already been found. If someone is in an unfamiliar city looking for a place to have lunch, and is standing outside a restaurant that has posted its menu by the front door, he must weigh the costs of delaying lunch and walking around a little further (the marginal costs) against what he perceives as the probability that some extra walking around will indeed reveal a better place to have lunch, times how superior the better restaurant is likely to be. If he is very hungry, or tired, and has a sense that there is unlikely to be much better on offer, and that even if there is something better it is unlikely to be *that* much better, then he will simply go into the restaurant at hand. We do intensive searches for a new house because we know (or should know) that there is a lot of variation in what will be on offer, and that the stakes are high – finding a better deal than the best looking purchase on hand can be a difference of tens of thousands of dollars. (On the other hand, housing search has the added marginal cost that continued search might cause one to lose the chance to buy what had been the best option.)

Everything in the search for a good deal is done at the margin: what would be the additional cost of search, what are the expected additional benefits. Marginal costs of search are typically increasing over time: we get tired of continued browsing, and delaying the purchase. And marginal benefits of search decline over time: the more we have already looked carefully at a large number of options, the lower the chance that continued search will yield an improvement over the best option already under consideration, and the smaller the likely improvement in quality and price if we do happen to find something better. We search until the marginal benefits of search have fallen and the marginal costs of search have risen to equal levels. To continue the search beyond that point would be to engage in an activity where the expected additional benefits are less than the additional cost.

Next, let us consider in turn two sorts of purchases: one where the consumer typically buys just one item meant to last for some time, and the decision concerns *quality* and price; and one where the consumer regularly purchases a somewhat standardized product, where the decision is more about *quantity* and price.

First, consider a consumer making a single, one-off purchase of an item; let's use stereo headphones as an example. Headphones come in varying styles and sound quality, and for each make that is on offer there is some level of satisfaction it will give the consumer above what they would have without the headphones. That level of satisfaction is the marginal benefit of the headphones. Each make of headphones also comes with a price. For the consumer, price represents the marginal cost of the purchase. For each consumer, the difference between the marginal benefit of the headphones and the price that is being charged is called *consumer surplus*, which could be thought of as the net benefits of the purchase. Each set of headphones on offer comes with an associated level of consumer surplus; some sets might even come with a negative estimate of consumer surplus, where the price is higher than any expected benefits. So, how do we apply our marginal-benefit/marginal-cost rule when there might be a few choices of headphones that offer benefits in excess of costs, but the consumer only wants to buy one headset?

The consumer will purchase the specific make on offer that brings the highest level of consumer surplus. (We will make much use of this theory in Chapter 6, where we look at price-setting of products of varying quality, such as seats in a performance hall, or editions of a book.) If there is no model of headphones in existence that generates a positive consumer surplus, then none will be purchased.

Here is another way to frame the headphones decision. As we consider different models, we notice that each upgrade in quality comes with a price attached to the improvement. If we look at models starting with the lowest quality and working our way up the quality ladder, we can ask at each stage, "Is the marginal increase in quality worth more to me than the marginal increase in price?" As long as the answer is "yes," we continue to look at higher quality models. But eventually most of us reach a point where the next upgrade in quality is not worth the additional price. At that point we have found the make we ought to buy, where the marginal benefit of additional quality is equal to the marginal increase in the price of extra quality. Connoisseurs of high-fidelity sound equipment, or wines, or olive oil, or fashion, will find their optimum at a higher level of quality than the choice of the ordinary buyer; for them, marginal benefits from quality improvements remain high even as the price goes beyond what most of us would be willing to pay. (We will see in Chapter 6 that the strategic arts manager will look for ways to offer varying quality levels, thus providing an option for each type of consumer.)

Now consider a different situation, where the consumer purchases multiple units of a standardized product each month – eggs, for example. The marginal cost to the consumer of purchasing eggs is the price of eggs. The marginal benefits of eggs purchased per month are declining; the more eggs I have eaten this month, the less interested I am in having eggs for tomorrow's breakfast.

Imagine a person who is at least interested in buying *some* eggs. If she has had none for a month, she would gain a lot of pleasure from being able to have one; the marginal benefit of that first egg, where there were none before, would be quite high. But if she has consumed 20 eggs this month, the marginal benefit of what is potentially the twenty-first egg is not so high. The marginal benefit declines as she has more eggs, until a point is reached where it falls all the way to zero, at which point this consumer would turn down the opportunity to have one more egg even if offered to her for free. How many eggs a month will she consume? She would purchase eggs up to the point where the marginal benefit has fallen to a level equal to the price of eggs (which, remember, is the marginal cost of eggs to her), but no more than that. To find the consumer surplus in this case, we need to find the sum of the surplus associated with each egg. For example, suppose it turns out that for this particular consumer the optimal number of eggs is 24 per month (it will be different for other consumers; some will buy more, some less, some will not buy eggs at all). Figure 2.1 shows the marginal benefit for each egg: for the first egg the marginal benefit is given by point A, for the tenth it is given by B, and for the twenty-fourth it is point C, which is also equal to the price of eggs, P.

For this particular consumer the consumer surplus from eggs is given by the area of the triangle ACD. This area represents the sum of the difference between marginal benefit and price for each egg consumed.

In Chapter 1 we introduced the concept of *reservation price*, which is the highest amount a consumer is willing to pay for something. For a single purchase, the most any consumer would be willing to pay is the marginal benefit they would receive from the good. Thus, consumer surplus is the difference between reservation price and actual price. This implies an interesting result for when a quantity of a good is purchased, such as in the case of our egg-consumer. In Figure 2.1, the triangle ACD represents the consumer surplus from buying 24

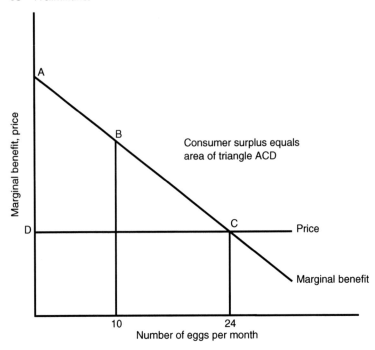

FIGURE 2.1 A consumer's marginal benefit from eggs

eggs. Now, suppose that stores did not offer the option of buying a single egg at a time, but eggs could only be purchased in cartons of 24. The reservation price for a carton of 24 eggs is given by the total area beneath the marginal benefit line from point A to point C.

The price per egg that this consumer would be willing to pay, if they could only be bought in cartons of 24, will be less than what she would be willing to pay for a single egg if she had none, but more than what she would be willing to pay for the twenty-fourth egg if she already had purchased 23. (This idea will be useful to us in Chapter 5, when we consider the problem known as "two-part pricing," and in Chapter 7, when we look at setting prices for subscriptions and memberships.)

Now let us tie all this to the demand curve that was introduced in Chapter 1. The demand curve tells us, for any given price, the total amount of customer demand for the good. Figure 2.2 uses the same example from Chapter 1: the demand curve for a concert. At any price, every consumer receives at least some consumer surplus except for the one who, at the going

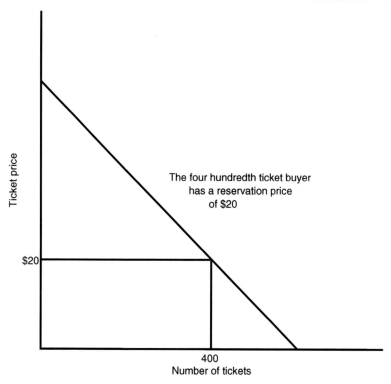

The four hundredth ticket buyer
has a reservation price
of $20

$20

400
Number of tickets

Ticket price

FIGURE 2.2 Demand curve for a symphony concert

price, was essentially paying their reservation price. Suppose, for example, the price is $20 and 400 tickets are expected to be sold. If the price were even slightly higher, demand would be slightly lower; there is one customer, the four-hundredth, who will pay as much as $20 but no more. Let us define the *marginal customer* as the one who has a reservation price equal to the actual price, and who would not make a purchase if the actual price were even slightly higher.

In Figure 2.2 the demand curve is a straight line, but it need not be so. The one thing we do know about its shape is its negative slope. A concept that will be useful to us throughout this book is *elasticity of demand*, which is defined as the expected percentage change in quantity demanded divided by a small percentage change in price. If a 2 percent increase in price would cause the quantity demanded to fall by 1 percent, then elasticity of demand around that price is 0.5. If a 1 percent decrease in price would cause quantity demanded to rise by 3 percent, then elasticity of demand around that price is 3.0. We say that when elasticity is less than one there is *inelastic demand*, and when elasticity is greater than one there is *elastic demand* (a rule of thumb for remembering which is which is to think of elasticity as measuring *responsiveness*: elastic demand is demand that is highly responsive to price, and inelastic demand is relatively less responsive to price).

Elasticity can be, but generally is not, constant as we move along the demand curve. Thus, whenever we talk about elasticity we are referring to elasticity around a particular price; elasticity might be different at a different price. If the demand curve happens to be a straight line, as in Figure 2.2, elasticity gets smaller as we move along the curve from the upper left to the lower right of the figure; as we get closer to a price of zero, cutting the price in half has only a small percentage effect on quantity demanded; at very low prices demand becomes very inelastic.

Now we will look at the behavior of sellers. We put off the problem of how sellers set their price for now; that is the topic of all the chapters that follow. However, there is something worth saying on the topic of prices at this point.

We know from casual conversation that prices in our economy are somehow determined by "supply and demand." We have just finished describing some features of the demand curve. Is it now time to construct a corresponding "supply curve"? No. In economic theory, a supply curve tells us the quantity of product that firms are willing to bring to market when they have no effective control over the price, but must simply take the market price as a given. The corn and soybean farmers that surround the town where I live do not get to choose the price at which they sell; there is a market price that is, for the individual farmer, non-negotiable. But arts organizations each provide a *unique* experience. One farmer's soybeans are indistinguishable from another's, but that is not true of museums, performances, and festivals. And, as such, arts organizations must *choose* their prices. There *is* a demand curve, that tells us the quantity of demand there will be at various prices, and understanding the demand curve will be crucial for arts organizations in setting their prices. But for arts organizations, there is no supply curve.

Imagine a potential buyer offering to pay a certain amount for a product. Sellers, like buyers, have a reservation price, although in the case of sellers it represents the *minimum* price they would be willing to accept for supplying an additional unit of the good. For sellers, the reservation price is equal to the marginal cost of production, in other words the additional costs that would be incurred by supplying one more unit. As long as someone is willing to pay an amount greater than marginal cost, it makes sense for the seller to supply the good, for the excess of price over marginal cost is profit, and we work under the assumption that sellers do not want to leave potential profit lying on the table, so to speak. But it would not make sense to supply an extra unit of the good if the price being offered by the buyer were less than marginal cost, since in that situation the seller would lose money on the additional unit, which would cost more to produce than the revenue it would bring in.

The difference between price and marginal cost is the *producer surplus* for that unit of the good (recall the difference between price and marginal benefit was the consumer surplus). We define *profit* as the difference between the total revenues and total costs of the organization, and we could think of the producer surplus on the last unit sold as the marginal contribution to profit of that unit; if the last unit was sold for $8 and it carried a marginal cost of $5, then profits increased by $3 as a result of that sale.

Does the total producer surplus measure total profit for the organization? Not quite. An arts organization faces two types of costs. *Fixed costs* are those costs that do not vary with the number of customers served. Think of all the costs of mounting a production that are independent of the number of people who end up attending the show, or of running a museum even if one day no one came to view the art. *Variable costs* are those costs that *do* vary with the number of customers, and this is where marginal costs come into the picture. Producer surplus covers the difference between prices received and marginal costs, but that is not total profit, because fixed costs must also be covered. Arts organizations typically run with very high fixed costs and low variable costs; producer surplus is needed in order to be able to cover those fixed costs. An entrepreneur trying to decide on whether to launch a new organization in the arts will be asking whether the producer surplus of the organization, once up and running, would be able to cover the fixed costs. If not, then the organization is bound to run at a loss, and starting a new organization might not be a wise move. We would expect a sector of the arts where producer surplus would easily cover fixed costs to be one that would attract new firms; entrepreneurs will see the opportunity to make some profit.

The term "fixed costs" refers to costs that do not vary with the number of customers served, but that does not mean that fixed costs never change. The salaries of full-time musicians are a part of the fixed costs of running an orchestra, since those salaries do not vary with the size of the audience, but salaries are still likely to be rising over time. In fact, it has long been noted that one of the major challenges facing arts organizations is that fixed costs, which consist mostly of salaries, will rise over time (even after being adjusted for inflation) even when the productivity of workers – the amount of output they produce – is not rising. This phenomenon is known as "cost disease." Technological innovation, and new and improved capital stock, across the economy lead to rising levels of average worker productivity, which is translated into rising wages. But the rates at which worker productivity rises over time are unequal across sectors; manufacturing, agriculture, and transportation have all seen great increases in productivity per worker over the decades, as labor-saving technologies have been developed and adopted, but in many parts of the service sector, especially those that rely on personal contact – such as education, personal services, many aspects of health care, museums, and the live performing arts – it is difficult to adopt new technologies that reduce the need for employees. Cars can be assembled by robots, but we are not yet at a stage where children can be taught by them, or patients in a health clinic can be examined by them, or *The Cherry Orchard* can be performed by them. Wages in all sectors rise with average levels of productivity, and the arts are in a situation of having to pay salaries that are competitive with other sectors even though productivity is not rising. Fixed costs are perpetually increasing, and that means that organizations need increasing amounts of producer surplus to cover fixed costs and remain solvent.

For the final section of this chapter we bring consumers and producers together. Figure 2.3 shows the demand curve for a product and its marginal cost of production. If the price is equal to R, then according to the demand curve M units will be purchased per week. Consumer surplus is given by the triangle AER, and producer surplus by the area REFG.

Suppose we begin at a price of R, and then start to lower the price towards S – the price where the demand curve intersects the marginal cost curve. The total amount of production and consumption of the good would then move towards N. Two things happen. First, there is a shift in surplus away from producers towards consumers. That is not surprising, as we would expect, with a falling price and no change in the pattern of marginal costs, that consumers are gaining and producers are losing surplus. For the M units that were originally being sold, we see that consumers gain and producers lose the area REJS in terms of surplus. Second, as price approaches marginal cost there is an increase in the *total* amount of surplus. The triangle given by EHF represents surplus that, when only M units were being sold, did not accrue to anybody, neither consumers nor producers. In fact, at price S we can see that *total* surplus – consumer surplus plus producer surplus – given by the area AHG, is maximized.

Here is a way to think about why it would be the case that a price equal to marginal cost maximizes total surplus. Suppose that instead of a system of

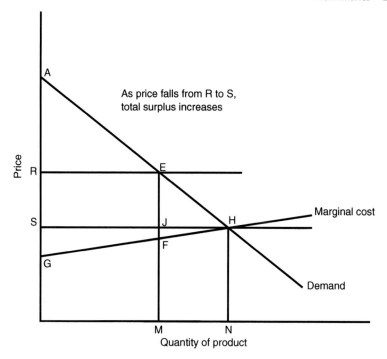

FIGURE 2.3 Consumer and producer surplus

buyers and sellers in markets determining how much of each good is offered for sale, we had an economic dictator. Imagine for the sake of argument that the dictator is benign, and would like to set a quota for the production of each good that maximizes the net benefits to society as a whole. If our dictator is not only benign but also knows some economics, then the amount of production to aim for will be the one that equates the marginal benefit of the good to consumers with its marginal cost of production. But that is what we have at level of output N. The demand curve represents the marginal benefit of the good to consumers, and at quantity N marginal benefits are equal to marginal costs. The dictator would not advise producing an amount greater than N, since for all the units beyond N the marginal cost of producing the units exceeds the marginal benefits of those units in consumption. Similarly, the dictator would not advise producing an amount less than N, because if that were the case there would be a missed opportunity; the production of a few more units would bring greater marginal benefits than the marginal cost of producing them. So amount N gets the production level just right for maximizing the total benefits of producing this good.

In the next chapter we look at the specific case of a seller setting just a single price. We will find that it is generally the case that total surplus will not be maximized, and that the quantity of the product sold is less than the level where marginal benefits to consumers equal the marginal cost of selling to them.

Sources

The analysis of why Hollywood releases movies that are bound to lose money for the studio is in Caves (2000). The technique of polling individuals to gain insights into the values they place on public amenities is generally know as the "contingent valuation method": a survey of its use in the arts is given by Noonan (2003), and caution regarding use of the method in arts policy is provided by Throsby (2003). The seminal article on "cost disease" in the arts is Baumol and Bowen (1965); two interesting retrospectives are Baumol (1996) and Cowen (1996).

3

SETTING A SINGLE PRICE

In Chapter 2 we stated the general principle that decisions are made by considering marginal benefits and marginal costs of actions. In this chapter we will apply that rule to the problem of how to set a single price that will apply to all buyers.

Consider the case of Paul, a ceramicist who makes bowls that he sells out of his own shop. The bowls he makes are all variations on a theme, all using the same materials and roughly the same size and quality. He wants to find a price to post in his shop that will apply to all sales. How will he go about applying the rule of equating marginal benefits and marginal costs? Marginal benefits and marginal costs of what, exactly?

Paul knows there is a demand curve for his bowls: for any price he could set there is a corresponding expected demand by customers. So he is really finding a solution for two numbers simultaneously: price and sales. The easiest way to solve the problem is to focus at first not on price, but on the optimal quantity of sales. We will ask what are the marginal costs and marginal benefits of trying to increase sales by one unit per week, and, as per the rule we set out in Chapter 2, look for that quantity where marginal benefits and marginal costs to Paul from increased sales are equal. When we have solved this, we simply have to look to the demand curve to find what price would generate a level of demand equal to what we have found to be the optimal level of sales. Let's now work through the calculations.

In order to find the profit-maximizing price, Paul needs two sets of data: the marginal cost of producing bowls, and the demand curve for bowls.

Marginal cost is something determined entirely within his studio and shop. Paul needs to calculate the increase in total costs that would arise from increasing the production of bowls. There are material inputs – clay and glaze – as well as increases, if any, in energy or other utility costs. There is also the cost of his time. This will be subjective. Paul will need to ask himself, "What is the minimum amount of money I would require in compensation for spending extra time in the studio making one more bowl?" The answer will be a function of earnings opportunities outside of the studio, and the value he places on time with friends, family, or other pursuits. As with our piano student Maggie, from Chapter 2, we expect that the marginal cost of time in the studio will be increasing the more time he is already spending there, as his valuable time in other activities becomes increasingly scarce. Remember that the cost of the studio itself, and all the equipment it holds, the cost of the shop, marketing expenses, and any other costs that do not vary when he produces a few more bowls, are not a part of marginal cost, and for the purpose of choosing a price for bowls they do *not* enter into the calculations.

The other data Paul needs regards the demand curve for bowls: how many bowls could he expect to sell each week at different prices? We should say at the outset, and this applies throughout this book, that it will simply not be possible to know the demand curve with precision. Paul can keep careful data on rates of sales when prices were altered, and observe on an ongoing basis prices charged in related, neighboring stores. But consumer demand will always be in flux to at least some degree, based on local economic conditions, tourism, the offerings of other sellers, and consumer tastes in terms of the art being put up for sale. And this is the case even where the product on offer – ceramic bowls – is not changing much in style from month to month. Demand is even more unpredictable for new conceptual art, plays, films, and books, as each of these is distinctive and may or may not catch on with buyers. Even with all the resources Hollywood studios can devote to forecasting box office returns for new film releases, there remains a very large margin of error come opening weekend. Cultural economists like to quote William Goldman's maxim about the movie business – "nobody knows anything" – as perhaps overstated but with more than a grain of truth: we can do our best to predict the demand curve, just as all business managers must, whether in the restaurant or dry cleaning or hair styling business, but we are always making estimates that are imperfect. Over time, managers use their experience to become better at forecasting demand at different prices, but nothing is certain.

The first two columns of Table 3.1 show Paul's best estimate for weekly demand for his ceramic bowls over a range of different prices (these numbers

TABLE 3.1 Demand for bowls from Paul's shop

Price	Weekly sales	Total revenue	Marginal revenue
$40	15	$600	--
$39.50	16	$632	$32
$38.50	17	$654.50	$22.50
$37	18	$666	$11.50
$34.25	19	$650.75	−$15.25

are for the sake of illustration, and should not be interpreted as saying anything definitive about the real market for ceramics!). In this example, the prices of bowls are clearly marked for customers, there is no haggling, and everyone pays the same price. If Paul wishes to increase the number of bowls he sells each week, he needs to lower the price. The third column of Table 3.1 shows the total revenue that would be obtained at each price, and is found by multiplying the price by the quantity of bowls that would be sold at that price.

The fourth column of Table 3.1 shows *marginal revenue*, the increase in total revenue as a result of lowering the price in order to sell one more unit per week. For example, suppose Paul had been maintaining a price of $39.50, and was selling 16 bowls each week. In order to sell 17 bowls per week, he estimates he would need to lower his price down to $38.50. Were he to do so, weekly revenue would rise from $632 to $654.50, an increase of $22.50. So the marginal revenue of the seventeenth bowl per week is $22.50.

But if the seventeenth bowl sells for a price of $38.50, why does total revenue increase by only $22.50? Why is marginal revenue so much lower than price? The answer lies in the assumption we have made, that all bowls sell for the same advertised price. So, when Paul makes a decision to lower the price in order to increase sales from 16 per week to 17, it is not just the seventeenth bowl that sells at a lower price; *all* the bowls will now sell at a lower price. If it were the case that he could somehow continue to sell 16 bowls each week at $39.50, as he had been doing all along, and sell the seventeenth bowl, but *only* the seventeenth bowl, at $38.50, then the increase in revenue would indeed be $38.50. But we have assumed he cannot do that, and in order to increase sales he needs to lower the one-price-for-all price. Keep this in mind throughout the book: at the heart of the various methods of strategic price-setting we will cover in all the remaining chapters is the search for ways to keep the price high for some buyers but to lower the price for selected individuals and purchases. We have assumed in this model that Paul cannot price discriminate, but we will relax that assumption in the following chapters.

Notice that marginal revenue can become negative: lowering the price to increase sales from 18 per week to 19 actually causes total revenue to fall from $666 to $650.75, and so marginal revenue at that point is *minus* $15.25. The fall in price needed to sell one more bowl is so large that total revenue falls as a result, even though the number of bowls sold has increased. *Marginal revenue is negative when demand is inelastic*; if the price decrease necessary to increase sales is such that the percentage change in price is larger than the resulting percentage change in quantity of sales (which you will recall from Chapter 2 is the definition of inelastic demand) then total revenue will fall with the price cut. In our example, a price cut of 7.4 percent (lowering price from $37 to $34.25) was needed to increase sales by 5.6 percent (increasing sales from 18 to 19 per week), and total revenue would fall as a result. On the part of the demand curve where marginal revenue is positive, demand is elastic: a percentage cut in price leads to a larger percentage increase in demand, causing total revenue to rise.

Now consider the key question we have posed: what quantity of output should Paul choose? The answer is that he should *choose the level where marginal revenue approaches marginal cost.* Marginal revenue tells us the benefit Paul will receive from increasing his output of bowls by an amount of one extra bowl per week, and marginal cost tells us the additional cost he will face in increasing output by one bowl. Suppose Paul had been setting a price of $40, and thus getting 15 sales per week. Should he lower the price to $39.50 and increase weekly sales to 16? Yes: the additional (marginal) revenue would be $32, and it would only cost him $20 to make the extra bowl. Well then, should he lower the price even further, to $38.50, so that he can sell 17 bowls per week? Yes: the marginal revenue from this action would be $22.50, and, again, it would only be costing him an additional $20 per week. Should he further lower the price to $37, so he can sell 18 bowls per week? No: the marginal revenue from doing so would only be $11.50 – less than the cost of making the additional bowl. So $38.50 is his best price, and he could expect to sell 17 bowls per week. The optimal price is found by lowering price and increasing sales up to the point where marginal revenue has fallen to the level of marginal cost, but not to increase the quantity and lower the price any further.

Consider the following dilemma. We know that it is impossible to perfectly forecast demand. Paul's choice of a price of $38.50 is based upon his best estimate of the relationship between price and quantity demanded, but it is only an estimate. At a price of $38.50 he expects to sell 17 bowls per week. What does he do one week when an eighteenth customer arrives, wanting to purchase a bowl at the posted price of $38.50? Put aside questions of whether Paul feels honor bound to make a sale, or wishes to increase goodwill in the community. Would the additional sale be *profitable*? The answer is "yes." The unexpected customer is willing to pay the posted price ($38.50), which is significantly higher than the cost of making the additional bowl ($20). So Paul will happily sell to the unanticipated customer who is willing to pay the price he has posted. Why then didn't Paul *plan* on selling 18 bowls per week, instead of 17? Because he thought, as it turns out, mistakenly, that to sell 18 bowls per week he would have had to lower the posted price to $37, which would not have been a sound decision. But if demand is higher than expected at the posted price, he is happy to sell.

In the arts, it is *always* the case that the profit-maximizing price is above marginal cost. Indeed, as we will see in the next example, marginal costs in many sectors in the arts are quite close to zero. With price above marginal cost, it always makes sense to sell to everyone willing to pay the advertised price, even when demand is much higher than anticipated. Why, after all, do arts organizations have marketing departments? It is because each additional ticket sold at the posted price contributes to profit: price is higher than marginal cost. As an exercise for the reader I will ask: what is the optimal amount of funding to devote to marketing, assuming there are diminishing marginal effects on ticket sales as the amount of marketing rises?

But let's go back to Paul. Now, suppose the marginal cost of producing bowls rises, to $30 per bowl. It might be because the cost of materials has risen, or it might be that the costs of Paul's time have risen – perhaps he has greater demands on his time at home, or has an opportunity to work in a second job. Again referring to the data given in Table 3.1, the new optimal price will be where marginal revenue approaches the new marginal cost, $30. This is where price equals $39.50, and 16 bowls will be sold each week (we expect). At this price, marginal revenue is $32, as close as we can get to the new marginal cost of $30. It is not worth lowering the price from $39.50 to $38.50, because the marginal revenue from doing so ($22.50) would be less than the marginal cost ($30) of producing the additional bowl. It is not a surprising result that an increase in marginal costs causes a rise in price and a corresponding decline in sales. Notice that the rise in price does not perfectly match the increase in marginal costs; in this example, an increase in marginal costs of $10 (from $20 to $30) led to a price increase of only $1 (from $38.50 to $39.50). Define the *pass-through rate* as the change in price of output as a proportion of the change in marginal cost. In this example, in the neighborhood of prices we are examining (i.e. around $39), the pass-through rate is 10 percent: the price increase was just 10 percent of the increase in marginal cost.

What if Paul's fixed costs change? Suppose, for example, the premiums for insurance on his studio and shop increase. These are fixed costs because the cost of insurance is independent of the number of bowls he produces. *Changes in fixed costs do not affect the optimal price.* If, with marginal costs of $20, Paul's best price to charge is $38.50, that remains true whether insurance premiums rise or fall. The best price to charge is the one where marginal revenue approaches marginal cost, and fixed costs do not enter that equation. This point is counter-intuitive, and often misunderstood by the layperson. Surely fixed costs must matter *somehow*?

Fixed costs matter in that they directly influence the profitability of the enterprise. Paul earns less profit when his insurance premiums rise. Since profitability is affected, fixed costs influence the decision whether to start, or close, a firm. When Paul made the decision to set up a studio and a shop, he had to ask himself whether the enterprise would be expected to earn a profit. If fixed costs are simply too high given the marginal costs and revenue he anticipates, the business might not be worth starting. Likewise, if the business is up and running but fixed costs are continually increasing, and the consumer demand for output at various prices is not changing, then the chances increase that the business will shut down. So it is true that fixed costs matter, in the decision of whether to open, and keep open, a business. But once that decision has been made, and the business is indeed going to *remain* in business, the optimal price to charge for output is independent of those fixed costs. Prices depend on the demand curve (which tells us marginal revenue for different prices) and marginal costs.

Now let us consider a second example of setting a single price, this time for a concert, a single show by a touring musician, where all seats are general admission.

In this case marginal costs are virtually zero: an additional patron coming to the concert to take a seat that would otherwise remain empty imposes no costs on the manager of the concert hall. Matters are complicated by the fact that the venue has a fixed capacity of seats; marginal costs of extra customers are zero until the show is sold out. With that in mind, we will look at two cases, one where the capacity of the venue is not a binding constraint, and one where it is.

Table 3.2 shows the demand curve over a range of prices. As with the earlier case of Paul the ceramicist, the key data for setting prices is how many sales could be expected for a range of different prices. When it comes to

TABLE 3.2 Demand for concert tickets

Price	Ticket demand	Total revenue	Marginal revenue
$20	600	$12,000	–
$19.50	625	$12,187.50	$187.50
$19	650	$12,350	$162.50
$18.50	675	$12,487.50	$137.50
$18	700	$12,600	$112.50
$17.50	725	$12,687.50	$87.50
$17	750	$12,750	$62.50
$16.50	775	$12,787.50	$37.50
$16	800	$12,800	$12.50
$15.50	825	$12,787.50	–$12.50
$15	850	$12,750	–$37.50

touring musicians, the presenter can get a sense of this from knowing the past history of demand for concerts by musicians of similar genre and popularity in the local market, and also the nature of the demand for tickets in other places for this musician on her current tour. Demand can never be known precisely, nothing in the arts can be forecast with certainty, but the manager can make the best of what data is at hand to produce a forecast.

Concert halls work with larger numbers of customers than ceramicists with a small shop, so in Table 3.2 I express demand for tickets in multiples of 25. In this particular case, the numbers are such that every decrease in price by $1 per ticket increases demand for the concert by 50 tickets, but in other examples (the numbers for the ceramic artist given in Table 3.1, for example) the data might not be so regular.

In this example, by assumption, marginal costs are zero – there is no extra expense to the concert hall in admitting more patrons. For museums, marginal costs are close to zero when they are relatively uncrowded, but as the number of visitors at one time increases, it may be that the density of people in the museum calls for additional security, and also that additional visitors impose the cost of making the museum experience less pleasant for all of the other visitors. We will consider the crowding problem later in this chapter.

For now, ignore the capacity of the venue; we will bring that into play later on.

The presenter wants to find the price where marginal revenue equals marginal cost. Marginal cost is zero, and we can see from Table 3.2 that marginal revenue turns negative beyond 800 tickets sold, which corresponds to a price of $16. We can see that this is also the quantity of tickets where total revenue reaches a maximum, at $12,800. It is always the case that total revenue is maximized where marginal revenue is zero.

If marginal costs are greater than zero (as they were for Paul the ceramicist), then it is *not* the case that prices are set where total revenues are maximized. With positive marginal costs, and following the rule of pricing where marginal revenue equals marginal cost, it must be that marginal revenue at the optimal price is also positive, meaning that some extra revenue *could* be earned by increasing output. But it is not worth expanding output beyond where marginal revenue equals marginal cost, because the additional revenue gained is less than the extra costs that will be incurred. Thus, prices should only be set to maximize total revenue when marginal costs are zero (as in the current example).

Now let's consider the capacity of the venue. Above, we found that the profit-maximizing price is $16, and we expect a demand for 800 tickets. If capacity is 800 or more, then $16 remains the best price. With capacity greater than 800, that will not change: capacity could be 800 or 1,000 or 1,500, and $16 remains the best price in terms of maximizing profits. Any effort to lower the price to fill empty seats will reduce total revenue, as beyond a quantity of 800 tickets marginal revenue becomes negative. If it is the case that the organization is pursuing a mission where prices are not just about making the most profit, and filling the venue is important for its own sake, then naturally the organization might look into charging a price less than $16 if capacity is greater than 800. But we need to realize that this will come at a cost, as such a strategy would lower total revenue. We will return to this question in Chapter 10.

Now let's suppose that capacity is *less than* 800. In this case it will make sense to depart from the general rule of pricing where marginal revenue equals marginal cost, and instead price should be set at the level that generates an expected demand for tickets equal to the capacity of the venue. For example, if the capacity is 700, then price should be set at $18. We can see how this makes sense: if only 700 tickets can be sold, and that can be achieved by setting a price of $18, it makes little sense to lower the price to $16. Doing so would generate greater demand for tickets, but it would remain a fact that only 700 could be sold.

Note in this case the presenter regrets the fact that the venue has a capacity of only 700. Total revenue at a price of $18 per ticket will be $12,600, less than the $12,800 that would be earned were the capacity 800. Of course, with different demand for different artists, it is bound to be the case that sometimes the venue's capacity is smaller than would be desired; it would not be a sound capital investment for a town to build a performing arts center designed for the profit-maximizing audience of the most popular artist that would ever perform there.

Let's sum up what we know about setting a single ticket price for performances. First, find the price and associated ticket sales where marginal revenue equals marginal cost (where marginal cost is typically very close to zero). If the resulting expected ticket sales are less than or equal to the capacity of the venue, then adopt the corresponding price. If the resulting expected ticket sales are greater than the capacity of the venue, then look for the (higher) price that would be expected to generate ticket sales equal to capacity.

For our final consideration in this chapter, we turn to museums. We are still working with the task of setting a single admission ticket, valid for one day, which will apply to all visitors.

The strategy of finding a price and expected number of visitors where marginal revenue equals marginal cost remains in place and, as usual, marginal revenue is discovered by generating an estimate of the demand curve. But what does marginal cost look like in a museum?

For a museum that is not very crowded, marginal cost is probably close to zero. There is no need for extra staff or security when a few additional patrons come to the museum. In such a case, finding that spot on the demand curve where marginal revenue equals zero will give the profit-maximizing price.

But, if the museum is crowded, such that any additional patron to some degree (it might be small) reduces the enjoyment experienced by other visitors, then marginal costs are *not* zero. *Congestion costs* are the costs imposed by an additional visitor on all the other visitors. It is important to note that even if the cost to each of the patrons from one more visitor is small, we need to add that cost over *all* of the visitors who suffer, and that might well generate a congestion cost that is not trivial. For an analogy on a larger scale, think of the cost that a single driver imposes when he enters a highway that is very congested and moving at a speed below the legal limit. Even if he only slows down the vehicles behind him by ten seconds in getting to their destination, the total cost he imposes is ten seconds times the total number of vehicles that he has slowed down, and on a busy road that might add up to a lot of minutes.

Still, if we had a museum that was purely interested in setting an admission fee that maximized profits, would it care about the crowding problem? After all, it does not represent a direct cost to the museum, such as having to hire additional labor or materials. Yes, it *would* care about the congestion cost, because as congestion rises, so the reservation price of customers – recall that is the maximum amount they are willing to pay to visit the museum – falls. And so congestion is not an issue that can be ignored.

By how much do reservation prices fall with congestion? It will be different for every museum, and a challenge to estimate, but there has been research on the subject. Economists David Maddison and Terry Foster used a "paired comparison" technique to estimate the marginal cost of congestion arising from an additional visitor to the British Museum. Individuals were questioned upon entering or exiting the museum, and were shown two photographs. The photographs would be of a specific location in the museum, but involving different levels of congestion, either very high (where a photo was found of a room at its most crowded), medium (the average level of people in the room at any given time) and low. They would then be asked a question like "Do you prefer the current scenario with free admission [and they would be shown a photograph of high congestion] or paying an admission charge of £6 [and they would be shown a picture of medium, or low, congestion]?" Different individuals would be shown different rooms and asked about their willingness to pay for a less crowded experience. From this Maddison and Foster were able to derive an estimate for the congestion cost imposed by a marginal visitor, and it was not small: £8.05.

Now suppose the price of entry to this museum were raised to reflect the fact that marginal costs from extra visitors are not zero, but positive. We can imagine five types of consumer: (1) one who used to visit the crowded museum, and who is pleased by the higher admission price because the smaller number of attendees makes the experience so much more enjoyable; (2) one who used to avoid the museum because of the crowds, but who will now attend; (3) one who used to visit the museum and who will still visit, but whose consumer surplus has dropped somewhat, since the lessening of the crowds does not matter so much to them but they don't like the price increase; (4) one who used to visit but who will now stop visiting, because of the increase in price; and (5) one who never visited before and still has no interest. Consumers of types (1) and (2) are pleased with the change, and those of types (3) and (4) are displeased (type (5) is indifferent).

The example raises a more general point: if a venue is crowded, some customers might *prefer* a price increase. We might find parking meters a nuisance, but it can be a greater nuisance to be unable to find a place to park when you are in a hurry. I am glad an admission fee is charged for state and national parks where I live.

This chapter has covered the most basic pricing problem: setting a single price. But it is a rare arts organization that has only one price posted. In the next chapter, we look at segmenting the market, and offering different prices to different groups of people.

Sources

"Nobody knows anything" is from Goldman (1983). The study of the costs of congestion at the British Museum is by Maddison and Foster (2003).

4

SEGMENTING THE MARKET

In this chapter, and through the rest of the book, we relax the assumption used in Chapter 3 that all customers must pay the same price. There are a variety of pricing strategies that involve price discrimination, and they are not mutually exclusive. This chapter introduces one such means of price discrimination.

I'm going to introduce terms here that I will also use in subsequent chapters, and divide the market into *strong* (S) and *weak* (W) consumers. Imagine two potential audience members, John and Clara. John is a regular attendee at your venue, is willing to pay a higher-than-average amount for admission (and perhaps for quality as well), and is not particularly sensitive to changes in the price you charge. He is one of the strong consumers. Clara is not a regular, is price-sensitive, and will more carefully consider whether to attend. She is one of the weak consumers. Price discrimination is about gaining what revenues we can from the strong consumers, while at the same time making an offer to weak consumers (that will *only* be used by weak consumers) that draws them into the venue, so long as they are paying a price greater than marginal cost. To use this strategy effectively, the price-setting arts manager needs to know something about the habits and preferences of the strong and the weak consumers for this arts organization's offerings.

This chapter considers one particular strategy, known as *direct price discrimination*, whereby strong and weak consumers tend to belong to identifiable groups, and the strong group is charged a higher price than is the weak group. By "identifiable" I mean that the seller can easily check whether the buyer belongs to the group receiving a particular price; for example students, seniors, military veterans, those on social assistance, residents of particular cities or countries, or those who have made past purchases from the organization.

As a first step, we need to know that it is, in fact, feasible to set different prices.

First, we need to have some information regarding the demand for tickets of different prices by each of the two groups. As always, we cannot know this perfectly. But whether the distinction in price is to be made between students and non-students, or for seniors, or for in-state and out-of-state residents, the price-setter must have some idea for each group of how demand tends to respond to price. Be aware that it is not enough to know whether one group generally has less spending power than another; that will have *some* influence on willingness to pay by the group, but other factors will be involved as well, such as their interest in the performance or exhibition you have on offer, and other cultural events in which they might be interested that compete with your own. If these other cultural organizations offer a discount to a specific group, of course that will affect that group's willingness to pay for what *you* offer. Place of residence might also be a factor. At time of writing, for example, the Art Institute of Chicago offers a 10 percent discount on memberships to those whose residence falls beyond a 100-mile radius of the museum; those who live some distance from the city will have fewer opportunities to make use of their membership, and so could be expected to have a lower reservation price for a membership.

Second, there must be some way to easily verify whether a customer falls into the group receiving the lower ticket price, such as a student identification card, or some proof of place of residence if that is the criterion. How this works can vary across different markets. For example, in Britain it is common for theatres to offer a discount to those on Jobseeker's Allowance. But in the United States it is a less common practice; in some quarters social assistance carries a certain stigma, and so the practice of offering such a discount and asking for proof of status may entail a degree of discomfort.

Third, there must be ways to monitor and prevent resale of tickets from individuals in the group that is offered the lower price to individuals who would otherwise pay the higher price. This is easier when tickets are bought at the door, but more difficult when there are advance purchases; in that case, tickets must clearly denote whether they are for members of one group or another, and there must be some method of checking identification on entry to the facility.

In terms of establishing whether a buyer is in fact a member of the group being offered the lower price, and in preventing resale, note that the more expensive the ticket, and the higher the differential in prices, the higher is the incentive for buyers to try to cheat the system. A young non-student has low incentive to claim student status to gain a 10 percent discount at a café, but a larger incentive to lie for a 50 percent discount on an expensive and popular concert, whether in order to attend himself or to sell the ticket at a mark-up to another non-student. And so as we move to look at strategies for direct price discrimination, keep in mind that the application is dependent on the system being enforceable, and that the ability to apply this technique comes with the above restrictions.

To show how to set prices for two identifiable groups, I use the example from Chapter 3 that illustrated how to optimally set the price for a single, general admission performance at a concert hall. The first three columns of Table 4.1 are the same as those given in Table 3.2, and we found, assuming that the marginal cost of seating additional patrons was zero and the capacity of the hall was not a constraint, that the profit-maximizing price was $16, with 800 tickets sold. That was the point where marginal revenue approached marginal cost, i.e. zero.

Now suppose the price-setter has done some market research, and has found that the total demand for tickets at each given price can be divided into two groups.

The fourth and fifth columns of Table 4.1 show how the demand for tickets is divided between the two groups at each price. Notice in this example that the weak buyers only begin purchasing any tickets at all when the price is less than $20. If it is feasible to set different prices for S and for W, how should we go about it?

TABLE 4.1 Demand for concert tickets

Price	Demand	Total revenue	Strong demand	Weak demand
$20	600	$12,000	600	0
$19.50	625	$12,187.50	620	5
$19	650	$12,350	640	10
$18.50	675	$12,487.50	660	15
$18	700	$12,600	680	20
$17.50	725	$12,687.50	700	25
$17	750	$12,750	720	30
$16.50	775	$12,787.50	740	35
$16	800	$12,800	760	40
$15.50	825	$12,787.50	780	45
$15	850	$12,750	800	50

For now, as we did in Chapter 3, let's first find the solution for the case where the capacity of the venue is so large as to be irrelevant. *The rule for setting the two prices, for strong (S) and weak (W), is to treat them as entirely separate markets, and for each group to find the price where the marginal revenue for that group equals marginal cost.* To give an analogous example, consider a publisher of books who sells editions in Asia and in North America, where the expense of shipping books is so high that no one would find it profitable to buy cheap books on one continent and ship and resell them at a higher price on the other side of the ocean. The publisher will set a price in Asia where marginal revenue in Asia equals marginal cost in Asia, and a price in North America where marginal revenue in North America equals marginal cost in North America. It is as if they were selling two entirely different and unrelated products.

Tables 4.2 and 4.3 use the information on demand by S and W from Table 4.1 to calculate the marginal revenue for each group. In Table 4.3, I have extrapolated from the data in Table 4.1 to find the range of prices most relevant for discovering where marginal revenue for the weak side of the market is around zero. Notice that for each market I have calculated the marginal revenue from lowering price in order to sell ten more tickets – it is important in constructing our estimates that we use the same unit of quantity increase in each side of the market, so that we are comparing like with like. This is true even though I have assumed that to increase ticket sales by ten one needs to lower the price by $0.25 in the strong market and by $1 in the weak market.

TABLE 4.2   Strong side of the market

Price	Strong demand	Strong total revenue	Strong marginal revenue
$20	600	$12,000	–
$19.75	610	$12,047.50	$47.50
$19.50	620	$12,090	$42.50
$19.25	630	$12,127.50	$37.50
$19	640	$12,160	$32.50
$18.75	650	$12,187.50	$27.50
$18.50	660	$12,210	$22.50
$18.25	670	$12,227.50	$17.50
$18	680	$12,240	$12.50
$17.75	690	$12,247.50	$7.50
$17.50	700	$12,250	$2.50
$17.25	710	$12,247.50	–$2.50
$17	720	$12,240	–$7.50

TABLE 4.3 Weak side of the market

Price	Weak demand	Weak total revenue	Weak marginal revenue
$15	50	$750	–
$14	60	$840	$90
$13	70	$910	$70
$12	80	$960	$50
$11	90	$990	$30
$10	100	$1,000	$10
$9	110	$990	–$10

We see that, for S, marginal revenue approaches zero (which is what we have assumed to be the level of marginal cost – that it costs virtually nothing to allow one more customer into the venue) at a price of $17.50, leading to S purchasing 700 tickets. It is not worth lowering the price below $17.50 for this group, as total revenue would fall; marginal revenue for prices below $17.50 is negative.

For W, marginal revenue approaches zero at a price of $10, and 100 tickets are sold. What do we notice about these results?

First, by segmenting the market and charging different prices to strong and weak consumers, total revenues rise. With a single price for all, we found the optimal price was $16, with 800 tickets sold, for total revenue of $12,800. By segmenting the market, and selling 700 tickets at $17.50 and 100 tickets at $10, total revenue is $13,250. Since there is no change in costs, market segmentation has led to an increase in profits. This is not surprising. Giving an additional degree of freedom to the manager of an arts organization, in this case gaining the ability to charge different prices to different groups strategically rather than only being able to charge one price to all customers, cannot in general make the organization *worse* off (after all, if it did there always remains the option of simply charging both groups the same price).

Now suppose an employee comes to you and asks, "Why are we selling to the weak market at all? According to the numbers, we can sell 800 tickets at $16 each; why are we bothering to sell 100 at the low price of $10 when we don't really need to?" How might you answer?

One possibility might be to ask about the marginal benefits and marginal costs of shifting away from the strategy of selling 700 tickets in the strong market and 100 in the weak market, to selling even more tickets in the strong market and a few less in the weak market. At 100 tickets, revenues from the weak market are $1,000. We could give that up, and just set one price. We know from previous calculations that the profit-maximizing single price is $16, which brings sales of

800, and total revenues of $12,800. Selling 700 tickets in the strong market at a price of $17.50 brought $12,250. So, by eliminating sales to the weak market at their price of $10, we lose $1,000 in that market, but only increase revenues in the strong market by $550 ($12,800 rather than $12,250). It is not a good strategy to give up on the weak market. If you don't sell in the weak market, and instead try to increase sales in the strong market, you have to cut the higher price by so much that the gain in revenues in the strong market does not cover what you lost by giving up on the weak market.

If someone asked a publisher, "Why sell your books at such a low price in A, when they sell for much more in B," she could answer, "But I am already selling the optimal amount of books in B, at the price where marginal revenue in B equals my marginal cost. A is a different market, and so I sell in A at a different price, so long as I can make a profit there." It is important for producers selling globally, who want to use market segmentation, that it is difficult for anyone to purchase the good in the low-price location, ship, and re-sell in the high price location; such arbitrage is sometimes referred to as a "grey market." Producers frequently lobby governments to put regulations in place that prevent cross-border shipments. For example, publishers can ask that bookshops in country A must sell copies of books printed in country A, and not shipped from another location (this was an issue in Canada when it entered into a free trade agreement with the United States, and publishers in Canada wanted to ensure that booksellers could not acquire titles for resale in the (lower priced) United States). In the United States, pharmaceutical companies have lobbied to prevent import of lower priced drugs from Canada.

Are consumers made better off by the introduction of direct price discrimination? At first glance, we would say that those in the strong market segment are made worse off, as the price to them has risen, while those in the weak market segment have gained, since price has fallen for them. Can we say anything about the gains or losses to consumers in aggregate? There is a lengthy literature spanning decades wherein economic theorists have tried to answer the puzzle of when consumers in aggregate gain or lose from this pricing strategy. In a (very small) nutshell, here is what we know.

To begin, we see in the particular example we have been working with that consumers as a whole are made worse off. There are two reasons for this. First, the total quantity of tickets sold has not changed (that will not *always* be the case, but it is in examples where the demand curves for the market segments can be illustrated as straight lines). Profits for the arts presenter have risen, and with the total number of tickets sold unchanged, those profits can only come at the expense of consumers.

The second reason is more subtle, but important for us to understand. In the model with just one uniform price, 800 tickets were sold at $16 each. Who received tickets? The 800 people who valued the performance at least as much as $16. Who did not get a ticket? All the people of the community who did not value the performance as much as $16. Once the tickets have been sold, we would not expect any secondary market. The people already holding tickets are the people who value them most highly. But now let's look at the case of direct price discrimination. Imagine two consumers, Sophia and Wendy. Sophia falls into what the presenter considers the strong market segment. Her reservation price is $16.50. With no price discrimination, she would have been one of the 800 who purchased a ticket for $16. But with price discrimination, her market segment faces a price of $17.50, and so she does not purchase a ticket. Wendy is a member of what has been identified as the weak market segment. Her reservation price is $12. With no price discrimination, she would not have purchased a ticket. But with a price of $10 being charged to members of the weak market segment, she does purchase a ticket and attend the show. Can you see the problem? Sophia values this concert more than Wendy does. But Wendy is attending and Sophia is not. In fact, if the two were to meet and start discussing the forthcoming concert, they might strike a mutually beneficial deal where Wendy sells her ticket to Sophia at some price between $12 and $16.50 (presuming Sophia can actually use a ticket purchased through the weak market, i.e. no proof of identity will be called for at the door). So the second issue with direct price discrimination is about which individuals end up with a ticket – it will generally not be the case, as it is with uniform pricing, that all tickets go to those who value them most highly.

But it is not *always* the case that consumers as a whole lose out from direct price discrimination. The economic theory for when consumers as a group gain or lose is very mathematically challenging, but the intuition is clear. We know that when market segmentation is introduced there is a segment of the market that gains (the weak side of the market) and a segment that loses (the strong side, which now faces a higher price). So what happens in aggregate must depend on the relative size of the gain to consumers on the weak side and loss to consumers on the strong side. Remember two concepts introduced earlier: elasticity of demand is the percentage change in quantity demanded as a proportion of a small percentage change in price (see Chapter 2); and the pass-through rate is the resulting rise in the price of output as a proportion of a small increase in marginal costs (see Chapter 3). It has been shown that total consumer surplus will rise with the introduction of market segmentation if the ratio of the pass-through rate to the elasticity of demand in the weak side of the market is the same or larger than in the strong side of the market. Since it is the weak side that has the higher elasticity of demand – in other words, on the weak side the quantity of tickets demanded is highly responsive to changes in price – then aggregate surplus will rise when pass-through in the weak market is significantly higher than in the strong market. It is in this case that segmentation would tend to lead to a more significant price decrease and quantity-demanded increase by the weak side of the market, and not such a large price increase and quantity-demanded decrease in the strong side. But this is a technical point, not necessary to the practice of actually setting different prices.

The examples we have considered so far assumed no capacity constraint. And we derived the result that when markets can be segmented, the optimal strategy is to treat the two markets entirely separately, and to find in each the price and quantity of ticket sales where marginal revenue in that market equals marginal cost in that market.

Now let's assume there *is* a capacity constraint. This complicates matters, because one more ticket sold in the strong market necessarily means one less ticket available in the weak market. How should we approach this?

To set the scene: suppose that the marginal cost of seating a patron remains at zero. Ordinarily with direct price discrimination, we would set prices for the two market segments where for each segment marginal revenue equals marginal cost, i.e. zero. Suppose this rule would generate a total demand for tickets in excess of capacity. Intuitively, we would guess that this means we ought to increase prices until we reach a point where total expected demand equals capacity; that's what we did with the problem in Chapter 3, when we considered the case where only a single price could be charged to all consumers. This intuition is correct – prices need to rise. But which price – the one we would have charged in the strong market segment, or the one we would have charged the weak segment?

The answer comes in two parts. First, if the marginal-cost-equals-zero rule produces total demand that exceeds capacity, then the new prices should be such that expected total demand equals capacity. To repeat a point we have made earlier, this cannot be achieved with perfection; there is always uncertainty in consumer demand. But the target should be a total demand for tickets that just equals capacity. To set the price any lower will generate a loss in revenue, since the extra demand generated by the lower price cannot (because of the capacity constraint) generate any additional sales. To set the price any higher also costs revenue. Remember, we are dealing with a case where following the rule of marginal revenue equals marginal cost would generate demand for admission beyond the capacity of the venue. Increasing price to the point where demand just equals capacity generates extra revenue. But raising price beyond that point would lose revenue; marginal revenue at that point is positive, and when marginal revenue is positive an increase in price produces a reduction in demand sufficient to cause revenues to fall – the decline in quantity sold has an effect that outweighs the increase in price. And so, if the demand for tickets at the price that would equate marginal revenue and marginal costs is at a level that exceeds capacity, increase prices to the point where expected demand equals capacity, but don't raise them any further.

Second, if we are segmenting the market we need to think about how to raise the prices in both the weak and the strong side of the market. The solution is to find a combination of prices such that marginal revenue is the same in each of the two parts of the market. With no capacity constraint, and with a marginal cost of zero, we set the two prices such that marginal revenue in each market also equaled zero. With a capacity constraint, we need to increase prices in each market, which will bring us into a range where marginal revenue is above zero, but to balance the price increases such that marginal revenue is the same on each side of the market.

What is the rationale for this rule? Remember that marginal revenue tells us the increase in total revenue that would result from a small decrease in price and increase in quantity of tickets sold, or, conversely, the fall in total revenue from increasing price and decreasing quantity sold. Let's imagine for a moment that you are selling in two markets, where marginal cost is zero in each market, and prices are set such that marginal revenue is *not* equal between the two markets; suppose it is higher in market A than in market B. And suppose there is a total capacity constraint such that you can only sell more in one market by decreasing sales in the other (as would be the case in selling tickets to a capacity-constrained concert, where selling more tickets to students could only be achieved at the expense of selling fewer tickets to non-students, for example). If marginal revenue is higher in market A, then think of what happens if you try to sell more tickets in market A (by lowering the price charged in A), and fewer tickets in market B (by raising the price in market B). The revenue gained in A from this move is higher than the revenue lost in B, given the differences in marginal revenue. Thus, I can increase my total revenues (with no change in costs) by selling more to market A and less to market B. If marginal revenues are unequal across markets, I can make adjustments to increase my profits. Now, eventually the gains from altering prices will come to an end. As I lower the price in A, marginal revenue in market A will begin to fall. And as I increase the price in B, marginal revenue in market B will begin to rise. When I reach the point where marginal revenue in the two markets is the same, there will be no more adjustments I can make that would increase total revenue; I will have arrived at an optimal balance between the two prices.

To illustrate, let's stay with the example we have worked with throughout this chapter. With no capacity constraint and direct price discrimination, we ended up with total demand equal to 800. Suppose capacity is only 700. Then, according to the numbers in Table 4.1, we would want to charge $19.50 in the strong market and $12 in the weak market. That would give us a combined total demand of 700 (620 from the strong market; 80 from the weak market), satisfying our first condition, and the marginal revenue at those prices is close to equal ($42.50 in the strong market; $50 in the weak market) between the two segments.

Consider: with a total number of seats at 700, selling 620 in the strong market and 80 in the weak market, ask "Could we do better by altering the balance of ticket sales between the two segments?" If the marginal revenue is close to equal in the two segments with the present division, then the answer is "No, we could not do better."

To see this, first suppose we try to sell more in the strong market and less in the weak. If we try to increase tickets sold in the strong market from, say, 620 to 630, we gain $37.50 in revenue from that market: total revenues from that side of the market rise from $12,090 to $12,127.50. And reducing sales in the weak market from 80 to 70 (as we must do if we increase sales in the strong market by 10) will lose us $50 in revenue in that segment (as revenues fall from $960 to $910). So that would obviously be a bad idea; we lose more from the cut in sales to the weak market than we gain from the increase in sales in the strong market.

Second, let's try going the opposite direction, selling less in the strong market and more in the weak market. If we decrease sales in the strong market from 620 to 610, we lose $42.50 in revenue; increasing the strong market price from $19.50 to $19.75 decreases total revenue in that side of the market from $12,090 to $12,047.50. And if we then make a corresponding increase in sales in the weak market, from 80 to 90, by lowering the weak market price from $12 to $11, we gain $30 on that side of the market, as weak side revenues increase from $960 to $990. But overall we have lost: this move has cost us $42.50 in the strong market to gain only $30 in the weak market.

If capacity is constrained, and we are segmenting the market, we cannot do better than to (1) price such that total demand across the two markets is equal to capacity, and (2) balance the two prices such that marginal revenue between the two markets is as close as possible to being equal (and remember to calculate marginal revenue in the same units across the two markets, or you will get incorrect results. In this example I have used increments of ten tickets as the common unit for calculating marginal revenue in the two markets).

If the marginal revenue formula seems too abstract, remember that the logic behind it is not so hard to apply. Suppose you have been charging one price to students, another to non-students, and that the venue frequently sells out. Then our rule asks that you check: would the revenue I could gain from trying to sell more tickets to students be larger than what I would lose from selling that many fewer tickets to non-students? If so, then you are not currently at an optimum, and should go ahead with making that adjustment. If not, try the other direction: is the revenue I would gain by trying to sell more tickets to non-students, through decreasing their price, higher than what I would lose from having to sell fewer tickets to students. If so, then make that adjustment. If not, if you cannot increase total revenues by making an adjustment in either direction, then you have the balance of the two prices about right. "Marginal" is simply a term for expressing small changes from the current state, and when you cannot improve upon revenues by making marginal changes, you are in a good position.

Sources

The literature on the impacts on aggregate consumer welfare from direct price discrimination has become quite mathematically sophisticated. But for the reader who wants more, the fact that with "straight-line" demand curves market segmentation will lead to no change in total sales dates from Pigou (1920). The effects on welfare were investigated by Joan Robinson (1933), and more recently by Schmalensee (1981), Varian (1985), Aguirre, Cowan and Vickers (2010), and finally, with the results presented in this chapter, by Cowan (2012).

5

TWO-PART PRICING

This chapter introduces the strategy of *indirect price discrimination*. Unlike the case in the previous chapter, we will now suppose that all customers face the *same* set of prices, where prices take on the look of a "menu," with offerings varying in quantity, quality, and other respects. From the seller's perspective, strategy involves setting the menu such that those from the "strong" side of the market effectively pay a higher total amount than those from the "weak" side, and this works even though we cannot easily observe who are the strong or weak consumers, and though all consumers are presented with the same menu of prices.

The first type of indirect price discrimination we will consider is known as two-part pricing. Most arts organizations are able to choose prices in addition to those set for admission. Drinks can be sold at intermission, souvenirs can be available for sale, museums might have special exhibits that require an additional fee beyond general admission, and movie theatres sell popcorn.

Being able to set multiple prices is a great advantage to arts managers, because it provides the freedom to effectively charge different total prices to different patrons. And if the manager does some digging into the behavioral patterns of different patrons, she can use the menu of prices to achieve the goal we have been working towards – gaining high net revenues from those patrons willing to pay more, while not losing those patrons only willing to pay a lower amount.

But before getting to that, let us consider a simple problem involving two prices, where in this case customers are for the most part alike; then we can deal with the two-part pricing problem with strong and weak customers later in this chapter. We will use an example first articulated by Walter Oi: an amusement park. Our two prices will be the price for admission into the park, and the price for each ride once inside the park. Either of these prices could be set at zero: there could be an entry fee but with all rides free (as at Disneyland), or there could be free entry but a price for each ride (as is the case at my local county fair), or there could be prices for both entry and the rides.

An assumption we will make for now, but relax later, is that we don't know much about the habits of our customers. Specifically, we know that there are some people who go to amusement parks who simply like the experience and atmosphere, but quickly tire of rides. There are others who go purely for the thrill of the rides, and they ride all they can. Who are the people who, in general, are willing to pay a high amount for a day at the fair: those who mostly like the atmosphere, or those who are primarily there for the rides? For now, let's say we are not really sure.

Customers will consider the two prices jointly when deciding whether to come to the park, and how many rides to purchase once inside. We will maintain the assumption we have used throughout this book: customers are reasonably well informed. Thus, they know the price of individual rides before they enter the park. The two-part pricing strategy is *not* based on surprising customers with high prices once inside (a strategy that would never work in the long run – everybody who attends a movie *knows* before entering the cinema that refreshments will be expensive; everybody who buys a printer for their home computer *knows* in advance that ink cartridges are dear).

It is best to solve this problem in steps: first we will look for the best price for rides, and then we will look at the price for entry.

An important consideration is that when people decide whether to come to the amusement park in the first place, they keep both prices in mind. The cheaper the rides, the more any customer will be willing to pay to get into the park.

Consider the *marginal cost* to the seller of allowing an individual on a single ride. Recall that this is the additional cost arising from just one more rider. In many cases marginal cost might be very near zero, but for the sake of illustration, suppose in this case it is $1. *The best strategy is to price rides at their marginal cost.* So in this case rides should be priced at $1. To show why this is so, let's consider in turn pricing rides at more than $1, and pricing rides at less than $1.

Suppose the marginal cost of a ride is $1, but the charge is $2 per ride once the customer has paid the entry fee to the park. Recall (Chapter 2) that customers will have *diminishing marginal returns* to rides; they will be willing to pay high amounts for the first few rides, but their willingness to pay for an additional ride will be falling with the number of rides they take. Eventually customers will reach a point where they say "I am not willing to pay as much as $2 for an additional ride," and at that point they start making plans to go home. Consider one such customer, Linus. Table 5.1 charts his willingness to pay for an additional ride.

Linus is willing to pay as much as $2 for his twelfth ride, but will only pay as much as $1.50 for the thirteenth. He will be willing to pay only as much as $0.20 for his fifteenth ride, and by that time is so tired that you would have to *pay him* $0.50 to induce him to take a sixteenth ride.

Let us focus on that thirteenth ride for Linus. It would cost the seller $1 to allow him to ride, and Linus values the thirteenth ride at $1.50. If the thirteenth ride were priced at $1, the seller should be able to induce Linus to pay up to $0.50 more to get into the park, since the thirteenth ride would have a net value to Linus of $0.50 (he pays $1 for a ride he values at $1.50). So, in selling the thirteenth ride for $1 the seller would collect an extra $1 in revenue from selling the ride and an extra $0.50 in revenue from admissions to the park. This means an extra $1.50 in revenue for the seller for a ride that only cost the seller $1 to supply. *Sellers are best off lowering the price of rides down to the level of marginal cost per ride, and recouping the surplus that customers gain from buying rides in the price charged for admission to the park.*

Does it make sense to lower the price of rides to something *below* marginal cost? No. Suppose the seller made rides free once people had paid for admission to the park. Linus would take 15 rides (from Table 5.1, he was willing to pay as much as $0.20 for the fifteenth ride) but no more. Linus values his fourteenth and fifteenth rides at less than the amount it costs the seller to provide them ($1 each). Linus values those two rides, in total, at $1.10 ($0.90 plus $0.20). If rides had been priced at $1, Linus would not have taken the

TABLE 5.1 Linus's willingness to pay for one more ride

Number of rides	Maximum he will pay for one more ride
11	$2
12	$1.50
13	$0.90
14	$0.20
15	−$0.50

fourteenth and fifteenth rides, and the seller would have reduced the value to Linus of the park experience by $1.10. Thus, the seller would need to reduce the admission fee by that amount to leave Linus just as well off. But lowering his entry fee by $1.10 is quite acceptable to the seller, because the seller now spends $2 less on providing what would have been those marginal rides to Linus. It doesn't make sense to charge Linus less than the marginal cost of rides, because he values those last rides less than it costs the seller to supply them. *Better to raise the price of rides up to the level of marginal costs and lower the admission fee in turn.*

So we have solved step one of our problem: set the price of rides equal to their marginal cost. There is a general principle at play in this solution. Any time a consumer values an additional unit of a good at some amount higher than the marginal cost to the seller of supplying it, there is a possibility of creating surplus by having that additional unit supplied and consumed. If for some reason that transaction does not take place, then an opportunity has been lost. Strategic sellers will look for ways to create any possible surplus, and in turn reap at least some share of that additional surplus for their own profit; colloquially, sellers will not want to "leave money on the table." The essence of so much of strategic pricing, as will be seen throughout this book, is to find ways to capture opportunities for surplus that remain "on the table" if the pricing scheme is a simple one of one single price and one item for sale applied to all customers.

Now let's return to our example. Once the amusement park has decided its price per ride, step two simply follows the techniques we have used in previous chapters for finding the best price of admission. A price per ride of $1 will generate a pattern of demand by customers in terms of what they are willing to pay for entry to the park, and the admission fee would be that price that equates the marginal revenue from the admission fee to its marginal cost (not the marginal cost per ride, but the marginal cost if simply admitting someone into the fairgrounds). Once the price per ride has been set, the best admission fee can be found by the methods described in Chapter 3.

There is a general principle at work in this example that is important for the arts manager to understand. Customers value "rides" – or visits to rooms in a museum, to take a similar example – more than it costs the seller to provide them; that's why the firm is in business at all. The difference between how much buyers value the good and what it costs to provide it is, as explained in Chapter 2, the "surplus" created by this good. Setting the price of rides equal to their marginal cost maximizes the total surplus created. It ensures that the number of rides taken is the one that equates the marginal benefit of rides to visitors to the marginal cost of providing them. It is in the seller's interest to set a price per ride that maximizes surplus, because the price charged for admission is dependent upon the surplus generated by rides. A higher surplus means more can be charged for admission.

With this in mind, consider a museum with many rooms, and suppose it is relatively easy to charge visitors per room if that were desirable to the museum management. If the marginal cost of letting an additional visitor into a specific room is zero, then it makes sense not to charge per room. Allow visitors as many rooms as they like, and capture the benefits to them of the visit in the general admission fee.

In a similar vein, consider a proposal recently advanced that museums might want to consider charging visitors according to the amount of time spent in the museum. Those visiting for four hours would pay more than those visiting for two hours. Does this make sense? If the museum is not crowded, then the marginal cost of a patron remaining in the museum for an additional hour is zero. In that light, it does not make sense to charge for additional hours. The museum's best pricing strategy is to allow unlimited time once inside, and to capture the benefit to visitors of having unlimited time through the admission fee. It can charge an admission fee and offer free "rides," which in this case are all the different rooms and exhibits, for as many hours as the visitor likes, or it could lower its basic admission price (perhaps all the way to zero) and charge per room viewed, or per hour of viewing. But for almost all museums, the marginal cost of allowing the customer to stay for another hour, or to visit additional rooms, is zero – no one imposes additional costs by staying for three hours instead of two. And so it doesn't make sense to charge visitors extra for that third hour. (Note there might be "special" exhibits where we depart from this rule; we will talk about these cases later in the book.)

The one exception that makes sense is where the museum is so crowded that a visitor staying an extra hour really does impose a cost – the museum is, as a result, more crowded for all the other visitors. As discussed in Chapter 3, in this case there is a significant marginal cost attached to a visitor's time in the museum, and a charge is appropriate for that time. But the museums that face that issue are few. For the vast majority, giving visitors as much time as they want under a single admission fee, even if they don't use it, makes sense.

Another example comes from television. A recent debate on public policy in the United States has centered on pricing for cable television. Those who subscribe to cable television know that even the most basic package contains a lot of channels, many of which most subscribers never intend to watch.

Where I live, the most basic package available has about 80 channels, offering a selection where it is impossible to imagine anybody watching all of them. Most people are going to spend most of their television-watching time on just a handful of channels. Why can consumers not have the option of just purchasing the few channels that they expect to actually watch? Is the problem a lack of competition among cable providers? That seems unlikely; if offering channels to customers à la carte were a good deal for viewers, we would expect that some entrepreneur would start a service that offers such a model. But that hasn't (yet) happened.

In cable television, channels are like the rides in our amusement park example – customers pay a subscription fee, and then can watch whatever channels are in that basic package for free, for as many hours as they like. As we have shown, this makes sense, as the marginal cost of providing those extra channels and viewing time to the customer is zero (it doesn't cost my cable provider anything if I happen to watch Jewelry Channel at 3:00 a.m. when I can't sleep). No one watches every channel, just as most people who go to Disneyland do not ride every ride, and I do not read every article in my *New Yorker* subscription (where the publisher sending me my weekly issue of the New Yorker, or offering me an online subscription, is like the amusement park admission fee, and allowing me to read individual articles within the issue is like offering rides, at zero marginal cost to the publisher). We pay the admission fee because of the channels, or rides, or magazine articles we do like, and find it worthwhile.

Pricing strategies are not mutually exclusive. Sellers can simply set a single price for admission according to the methods we outlined in Chapter 3, or offer concessionary prices as per Chapter 4, and/or premium prices for VIP treatment (say the ability to jump the queue for rides) as we will describe in Chapter 6, and/or discounts for multiple admissions as will be covered in Chapter 7. All these techniques apply in the same way once the price per ride has been set.

Now recall that at the beginning of the chapter we made the assumption that we do not have much information about the intensity of preferences for "rides," relative to the intensity of preference for simple "admission," among strong and weak consumers. Do strong consumers tend to be the ones who highly value rides, or are they most interested in admission, with little use of rides? Now let's relax that assumption, and suppose we do know something about strong and weak consumers. In this case, we will see that it might be strategic to depart from our simple case rule of pricing rides at the marginal cost.

Let us consider each of the possibilities in turn.

The first possibility is that the people willing to pay the most for a day at the fair are the ones who love rides. Those with a lower willingness to pay, who are somewhat on the fence when it comes to deciding whether or not to go to the fair, are generally those who have more interest in taking in the atmosphere but tend to go on few rides, even if they are low priced.

A thread throughout this book is that we want to find ways to get those willing to pay a high amount to actually do so, but not in a way that will lose those potential customers with only a low willingness to pay. And in this case the solution would be to depart somewhat from our simple case rule, by increasing the price on rides, and lowering the entry price. Why?

The intuition is as follows. First think about our weak market, on-the-fence customers with a low willingness to pay. They are pleased by the lower entry fee, and so are more likely to come to the fair. They don't care so much about the increase in the price of rides, because they don't tend to go on many rides anyway. The higher price on rides will generate revenue for the seller because the strong market customers with a high willingness to pay are going to buy a lot of rides. Even though we have lowered the entry fee for all, including for these customers with a high willingness to pay, sellers will earn money from them on the rides.

There are many examples where we can see this application of two-part pricing in action.

Consider printers designed for household use. As everyone who owns one surely knows, printers are almost surprisingly cheap (they can be found for under $100 in my town), but ink cartridges are expensive. The pricing strategy is that households, or small businesses, who are willing to pay a lot for the convenience of having a household printer are most likely to do a lot of printing. Households that are on the margin of whether or not to buy a printer are generally those who would do only small amounts of printing. The printer is like the admission fee to the amusement park, and ink cartridges are like rides. The low price for the printer itself (although a price still greater than the cost of producing it) allows the firm to make a sale to households who are not willing to pay a high price for the convenience of owning a printer. The high price for ink cartridges is the means of extracting significant revenue from those households who highly value having a printer; they will use the printer frequently, and therefore have to replace cartridges often.

Restaurants tend to set prices for their main courses at a relatively small mark-up on marginal cost relative to the mark-ups used on appetizers, drinks, and desserts. This is another example of two-part pricing where it is seen that the strong side of the market has a strong preference for "rides," in this case the extras that one can order with a meal, while the weak side of the market is simply looking for a good price on the main course, and will order little else. The price on the main course is kept low to entice the weak consumers into the restaurant, and strong consumers pay a high total price from purchasing wine and appetizers to go with the meal.

To take another example, it is a commonplace observation that refreshments at the local cinema are very highly priced. Why is that so? The layperson's response might be, "Well, once a patron has gained admittance into the cinema, there are no choices about where to purchase refreshments, and so the patron is at the mercy of the cinema owner when it comes to pricing." But is that answer convincing? As we noted earlier, anyone who goes to the cinema expects high prices for refreshments. And since a film showing is typically only about two hours long, it is surely possible for most viewers to have a meal or a snack or a drink before entering the cinema, which could satisfy them until the movie was over. The answer lies in an application of two-part pricing. Research has shown that the strong market for cinema, those who love to attend the movies on a regular basis, with a high willingness to pay, are also the patrons most likely to purchase refreshments from the cinema's concession stand. The weak market for cinema, the occasional patron with lower willingness to pay, tends to be less likely to purchase concessions inside the cinema. In this case, the rational strategy for the cinema owner is to keep admission prices reasonably low (in order to attract weak market patrons), and to gain revenues from strong market patrons at the concession stand, where they seem to be quite willing to pay the very high prices.

The popcorn example is useful in illustrating another consideration. The owner of the cinema is able to use the strategy of two-part pricing as a result of her owning both the screens where the movies are shown and the concession stand. Take as a counter-example the case of an outdoor movie screening where one person owned the right to sell tickets to watch the movie, but someone else owned a stand selling snacks and drinks, and where customers could make purchases at the snack-and-drink stand and take them into the grounds to watch the movie. The seller of movie tickets would price those tickets in a way that maximizes profits from the movie, all else being equal, while the owner of the snack-and-drink stand would set her prices to maximize profits from those sales, given the price of the movie. But this will not maximize the *joint profits* of the two enterprises. The owner of the movie showing would increase price above what would be charged by a single owner owning both enterprises, since an owner of the movie showing alone has no incentive to give strong market customers such a low price for admission, with no chance to recoup revenues from them elsewhere. The higher price for the movie showing lowers the prices that the snack-and-drink stand owner can charge for concessions. The two owners could do better of they somehow coordinated their prices, and subsequently share in the increased aggregate profits. But the law does not favor such collusion, and even if it did it is not costless for two separate owners to negotiate a coordinated approach to pricing. Thus, where the application of two-part pricing would be particularly profitable, we expect to see a single owner of the two goods for sale, not two separate owners.

Indeed, we can observe conflicts in pricing at cinemas owing to the (complex) arrangements that cinema owners and film distributors have for sharing box office receipts. If the film distributors claim a share of box office, but not a share of sales of refreshments, then the distributors would prefer that admission tickets were set in a way that would maximize revenues from admission sales. That would maximize the return to distributors. But cinema owners are not out to maximize revenues from ticket sales; they are out to maximize the total profits from ticket sales combined with concession sales. Strategic pricing leads them to hold down the price of tickets, but this conflicts with the goals of distributors.

In sum: if two-part pricing is to be used it is significantly easier to apply when a single owner is responsible for both of the prices, and conflicts may develop when two firms are sharing the revenues arising from one price and the firm setting the price is doing so in the context of its own two-part pricing strategy.

Now let's consider cases where the strategy dictates cheap rides and expensive admission. We would apply this "Disneyland" strategy when the strong market customers are more interested in simply "being there" rather than in taking advantage of all the rides on offer, but the weak market customers are particularly drawn by the rides. In this case, the seller uses the low-price rides to lure weak market customers; they are willing to pay the high admission charge because of the cheap rides once inside. And, of course, strong market customers are willing to pay the high admission fee simply because of their high willingness to pay for entry into the fairgrounds.

An interesting example comes from the case of music downloads. A team of economists looked into the standard pricing model for downloads, which essentially involves free admission, and a relatively high price per song ($0.99 or more). Is that a good model? It was found that an entry fee to a downloading service combined with a lower price per song would generate more total surplus. It suggests that the strong market for music downloads wants the option of downloading but would actually not purchase that many songs, while the weak side of the market would happily pay the entry fee in exchange for a lower price per song; the consumers with a generally low willingness to pay for the service would in fact use it a lot if the price were right. (As an aside, it is difficult to simply analyze markets for downloads of songs or books since there is the added complication of sales of necessary hardware, and competition for market share. Amazon.com has complex goals in the prices it sets for Kindle e-book readers and the e-books themselves.)

We could summarize the two-part pricing strategy as follows. If you do not have a good sense of the difference between strong and weak market consumer behavior when it comes to distinguishing tastes for simple attendance and tastes for extras, then price the extras at marginal cost, and use standard optimizing pricing techniques for admission, knowing that demand for admission depends upon the price you have set for extras. If you do know there are differences between strong and weak market consumers, then price extras below marginal cost (and in turn raise the admission fee) if weak market customers are especially attracted by the extras, and price extras above marginal cost (and in turn lower the admission fee) if it is strong market customers who are especially attracted by the extras.

Sources

The "Disneyland Dilemma" was analyzed by Oi (1971). Pay-as-you-go pricing for museums is suggested by Frey and Steiner (2010), and a useful introduction to the pricing of cable television is provided by Hazlett (2006). Gil and Hartmann (2009) explain why popcorn is expensive at the movies. Shiller and Waldfogel (2009) apply two-part pricing to music downloads.

6
PRICING QUALITY

In the previous chapter we introduced the concept of indirect price discrimination, in which all consumers are offered the same set of prices, but they make choices such that "strong market" consumers pay a higher total amount to the seller (as by definition they are willing to do), and "weak market" customers, but *only* weak market customers, pay less, albeit an amount that still adds to the profit of the seller (i.e. they are paying a price above the marginal cost of the service they receive). In this chapter we discuss a second method of indirect price discrimination, where the seller offers goods and services of different quality levels to consumers, charging more for the higher quality options. The practice is commonly observed: automobile, appliance, and consumer electronics manufacturers produce different models of varying luxury and price, couriers offer different speeds of delivery for different prices, airlines offer different classes of seats, and clothing companies produce premium and discount brands. In the cultural sector, performing arts venues "scale the house," charging different amounts for different quality seats, publishers have hardcover and paperback versions of books, record companies produce "deluxe" editions of CDs along with standard fare, and cinemas charge different amounts according to the day of the week and time of day. The practice is common; in this chapter we see if it is possible to think about setting prices for different qualities in a systematic way.

We begin with recognition that people have different willingness to pay for higher quality. When a publisher sets different prices for hardcover and paperback books, it knows that some customers will choose one and some will choose the other. We know different preferences are out there – what makes this situation different from direct price discrimination is that we cannot easily group people by preferences. Indeed, many individuals will be considered strong consumers in some markets and weak consumers in others. This may be the case even within a genre; for example, I might have a favorite author whose books I always want to acquire in hardcover, but I am content with paperback books for other authors. For some touring musicians it might be important to me to get the best seats I can, even at a very high price, while for other musicians I am perfectly fine sitting in the balcony.

Can the seller simply follow the rules we set in Chapter 4 for direct price discrimination? For any particular artist performing in a venue, why not estimate the demand for the lower quality seats, the demand for the higher quality seats, and for each type look to where marginal revenue equals marginal cost? As a thought experiment it is a good place to start. But this situation is different from direct price discrimination: the two sets of demands are interdependent. The demand for high-quality seats depends, in part, on what is being offered in the low-quality section. If the low-quality section is really not *that* bad, and if the price of low-quality seats is quite low, then some people who otherwise might buy a high-quality seat will pick the low-quality offering instead. With direct price discrimination, say between seniors and non-seniors, customers do not get to choose their age when purchasing a ticket – they are in one category or the other. But with quality differentials, individuals do have a choice to make in terms of which quality level is best for them.

To begin, let's start with a case where the seller is offering tickets to a concert at two different quality levels. We will take the quality differential as a given for now; later in this chapter we will look at how sellers strategically alter the quality levels of their products. For a seller to ask whether it has optimally set the price differential between high and low quality, it can examine the effects of changes at the margin.

First, let's consider the lower priced, lower quality seats. If this were the only type of seat available, then we know that the optimal price is where marginal revenue (the change in total revenues from slightly lowering the price in order to sell one more seat) equals marginal cost (the cost of seating one additional customer; for performing arts venues this is probably close to zero). In the case of two different qualities of seats on offer, the principle of optimizing at the margin continues to hold, but the analysis is slightly more complex. Consider what happens if the price of low-quality seats is lowered. First, there is the effect on revenue from gaining additional customers who otherwise would not have bought a ticket at all, offset by the fact that all low-quality seats are now selling at a lower price. That is the usual way we have been thinking about marginal revenue. But in this case there is an additional effect: some customers who had previously been willing to purchase a high-quality seat might switch to buying a low-quality seat now that the price is lower. A customer might have preferred an orchestra seat when they were priced at $25 and the balcony was $18, but if the balcony price falls to $12 the customer might switch from orchestra to balcony. And, presuming the marginal cost of seating a customer in one type of seat is the same as the marginal cost of seating him in any other seat, customers switching from high-quality to low-quality seats represent a loss in revenue to the seller. Taking the sum of these effects, the low-quality seats are optimally priced when, at the margin, the gain from slightly lowering the price, through bringing customers into the venue who otherwise would not have attended, is just equal to (1) the loss from lowering the price for all those already willing to pay the going rate for low-quality seats, plus (2) the loss from customers who previously would have purchased a high-quality seat now switching to purchasing a low-quality seat. If we do not have equality between these marginal gains and losses, such that lowering the price of low-quality seats would bring more gains than losses, then the price should be lowered. In that case, we would eventually find a price where the equality holds: as we lower price, the marginal revenue from bringing into the venue new customers is falling, and there will be an increasing number of customers who previously would have purchased high-quality switching to low-quality seats. When the marginal gains from lowering the low-quality price even further just equal the marginal losses, we have found the optimal low-quality price.

Now let's turn to the price of high-quality seats; how does the seller know it is set optimally? Again, look to the margin. If the price of high-quality seats were lowered slightly, the effects would be (1) those who were previously willing to purchase high-quality seats would continue to do so, although now at a lower price than before, which represents a loss to the seller, (2) some customers who previously were purchasing low-quality seats will change their minds and purchase a high-quality seat now that the price is lower, which is a gain, and (3) some customers who previously would not have purchased any ticket at all will be induced to purchase a high-quality ticket, which is a gain. If the high-quality ticket is priced optimally, then with a change at the margin it should be the case that the loss (1) would be just offset by the gains (2) plus (3), such that there is no net gain to be had from lowering the price. If it turns out that there *is* in fact a net gain to be had from lowering price, the seller should do so.

Another way to think of the above analysis is as follows. If the difference in quality levels is taken as a given – say, for example, the difference in quality between seats in the orchestra and seats in the balcony – then the seller wants to set balcony seats at a price low enough to entice the weak market consumer, but not so low that too many strong market customers who would otherwise have bought seats in the orchestra now decide that the balcony offers the best value. And the seller wants to set the orchestra price high enough that it captures the high willingness to pay from the strong market consumer, without being so high that, again, the strong market consumers either switch to preferring balcony seats, or decide not to attend at all. Even if strong and weak market customers have very different reservation prices, the price differential cannot become *too* large, as that will cut too deeply into demand for the higher quality option. There are two differentials in play: the differential in quality levels, and the differential in prices. They are linked; a significant difference in prices can only be sustainable when there is a big enough difference in quality. Otherwise, too many strong market consumers will simply opt for the low-quality option. If the difference in the quality of experience of sitting in the orchestra or the balcony is small, that limits the degree to which prices can differ, since too high a price differential will simply induce nearly everyone to purchase a balcony ticket.

The fact that the amount of the price differential is constrained, even if willingness to pay in the strong market is *much* higher than in the weak market, is a part of the explanation for why so many arts presenters are nonprofit organizations. Consider this example: suppose the total amount that customers would be willing to pay for a season of opera, adding the reservation prices of all potential consumers, is high enough to cover the costs of producing the season. In other words, the opera season is worth doing purely for the attendees alone, even before considering any benefits to the wider community. But there is no way that price discrimination can capture the full amount that different consumers would, in theory, be willing to pay. Segmenting the market between students, seniors, and those paying full fare, using two-part pricing for additional goods and services within the opera hall, and using price differentials for different quality of seats cannot capture the fact that, for some patrons, the opera season is worth thousands of dollars. A few wealthy opera-lovers would be willing to pay a very large amount to ensure the production of an opera season, but there is no way to price tickets to capture that. But the nonprofit form allows for "voluntary" price discrimination in the form of donations. Donors know that their contributions to the opera company will be devoted to opera, as by law nonprofit organizations cannot simply distribute net earnings to owners or managers. Charitable donations are the only way the opera company can capture the very high value that some patrons place on its art, such that costs can be covered. While this book is devoted to the myriad ways in which arts organizations can increase their revenues through strategic pricing, in some cases what can be raised through even quite sophisticated pricing schemes is not enough to capture the entire value that patrons place on the art, or to cover total costs. We turn to the question of whether nonprofit (and public) arts organizations ought to price for profit-maximization in Chapter 10.

To this point we have assumed that the quality differentials that are offered by the arts presenter are given. Orchestra and balcony seats simply offer a different experience for the consumer, and cinemas cannot do much about the fact that Tuesday nights are less popular for attending the movies than Friday nights. But there are many situations where the quality differential is not simply a given, but can be adjusted by the seller. Sometimes firms will *deliberately* lower the quality of the inferior good in order to maintain demand for the premium product.

Suppose a courier offers customers two levels of service – overnight delivery and two-day delivery – with a higher price for overnight delivery. If customers, through experience, began to find that it was often the case when they purchased two-day delivery that the package was in fact delivered the very next day, they have much less incentive to purchase the higher priced guaranteed-overnight delivery the next time they have a time-sensitive package to send. Why pay for overnight when paying for two-day delivery gets the package to the recipient overnight in any case? As a consequence, the courier has an incentive to delay delivery of two-day packages until the second day even if the package has arrived in the destination city overnight; in such a case the package can be held in the storage facility until the next day. This maintains an effective quality differential (if you pay for two-day delivery, two-day delivery is all you will receive) that enables the courier to maintain the premium price for overnight shipping. And this is so regardless of cost differentials. If a two-day delivery was purchased on Monday, but the package arrives in the destination city early on Tuesday morning, there is no cost differential to the courier in delivering the package to the recipient on Tuesday or on Wednesday. Indeed, it costs the courier *more* to deliver on Wednesday since that means the package takes up space in the storage facility for a day. But it is worthwhile as a means of enabling price discrimination, and ensuring that strong market buyers who really do need fast shipment keep paying the premium price.

In the early 1990s, companies introduced low-cost printers for household computers. Households typically are the "weak market" for printers relative to "strong market" businesses, who need to print more documents (recall our discussion of printers in Chapter 5 on two-part pricing, explaining why printers themselves are relatively inexpensive but ink cartridges are not). IBM's LaserPrinter was popular with businesses. The new household model, the LaserPrinter E, was very similar to the original LaserPrinter, except that it printed at about half the speed, and was priced at about 60 percent of the original LaserPrinter. The differential was not because the faster model contained parts that the slower model did not. Indeed, the opposite was the case: chips were added to the LaserPrinter E to deliberately slow it down. The slowness created a quality differential that would enable higher prices to be charged to the strong market buyers who valued the higher speed of the original model.

But if commercial couriers and computer manufacturers employ the strategy of deliberately reducing the quality of the lower priced option, would we ever see this in the arts? We do.

Consider hardcover and paperback books. There is, of course, a cost differential to the publisher. In common with virtually all genres of art, there are high fixed costs in production (the costs of writing, editing, typesetting, and marketing the book) with fairly low marginal costs of actually producing additional bound copies. The binding costs of a hardcover book, are, according to one estimate, about $3 whereas it is slightly less than $2 for a paperback. This small cost differential is not enough to account for the significantly larger differential we see in hardcover and paperback prices, which is driven by price discrimination between strong and weak market consumers. But what is interesting is not just that paperbacks have weaker, less durable (and, to some, less attractive) binding, but that the release of the paperback is delayed, sometimes for over a year after the release of the hardcover version. This represents a differential in quality – namely in the wait that is required to obtain the book – that is deliberately set by the publisher. If the paperback and hardcover versions were released on the same day, we can imagine many strong market customers, those who had been anxiously awaiting the book, would simply buy the paperback version. But the delay in the release of the paperback induces many strong buyers to opt for the hardcover version instead. Movie studios delay the release of DVDs until months after the film has shown on big screens, for the same reason; it buttresses strong market demand for seeing the film immediately upon release, a demand that would be diminished were the film to be immediately available for home viewing.

Why is it that half-price day-of-show tickets to Broadway theatre in New York City cannot be purchased by telephone or online, even though the mechanisms for buying tickets that way are already in place for other customers, and could easily and cheaply be employed by the theatre? Buyers are forced to go in person and queue because that makes these tickets less appealing to strong market consumers who might otherwise wait for the day-of-show to buy them. One econometric study found that theatres were offering a deal that was *too* good at these half-price booths; it was attracting too much demand, at the margin, from customers who would otherwise pay full-price for advance sales. The study estimated that something on the order of a 30 percent discount, not 50 percent, would in fact be profit maximizing.

Sometimes we see price differentials tied to the convenience of purchase even when the product itself is the same for all customers. Consider coupons that are made freely available that consumers can use at grocery stores to obtain discounts on particular items. The items purchased are available to all buyers who come into the store, but only customers willing to devote the time to collecting the coupons, and accept the inconvenience of remembering to bring them to the store, receive the discount. Coupons are a means for the store to offer discount prices to weak market customers, by creating an inconvenience that only those customers will accept. Strong market customers of the store will not bother with the coupons; that is by design. Rebates on purchases on electronics or appliances, where the consumer has the option of filling out a significant amount of paperwork in order to receive the rebate from the manufacturer, are of a similar nature; the offer is available to all buyers, but only a certain number will actually exploit it. The rebate draws weak market customers into making a purchase, while strong market customers pay full price by not caring to do the work that earns the discount to which they are entitled.

Note that in one respect we see an absence of price differentials by quality: arts organizations routinely charge the same price for each of their offerings even if some are going to prove more popular than others. Publishers charge roughly the same price for *all* their works in a particular genre (say, literary fiction, for example) even if some are going to prove to be much more popular, or critically acclaimed, than others. The same is true for performing arts organizations, cinemas, and so on. Why not price discriminate on the basis of higher quality books, shows, or movies? The answer lies in the fact that the seller does not want to indicate a quality difference in the *content* of the art, as it would decimate demand for the lower quality offerings.

For many cultural goods, the primary cost to the consumer of the good is the time required to experience it. If I purchase a new hardcover novel for

$25, the cost to me in the hours spent reading it will greatly exceed $25, and my frustration with a disappointing book is not going to be that I spent $25 to acquire it, but that I wasted so many hours that could have been devoted to another book or another activity. The $10 I pay to see a movie on the big screen, the $20 I pay to see a play at a local theatre, are outweighed by the hours taken up in getting to and from the venue, watching the show, and perhaps even the direct cost of child care.

Cultural goods are experience goods, and every customer is taking something of a small gamble in going to a live performance, a museum, a film, or in purchasing a book; the customer cannot know how much she will enjoy the art until she has actually done so. The cultural economy thrives because so many people are willing to take these gambles, on the basis that the "wins" from experiencing meaningful, enjoyable art exceed the "losses" from attending a disappointing show or exhibition. Because there are so many cultural goods on offer, of which each consumer, even an arts lover, can only have time to sample a small portion, any offering where the seller suggests that it is of lower quality will quickly have demand sink close to zero. Were publishers to begin differential pricing of novels based on their own perceptions of the quality of the novels, there would be very few customers for the lower priced novel; what reader would choose what the publisher suggests is a mediocre book in order to save a few dollars?

Where we do see differential pricing it is based on quality differences that the consumer can easily observe and understand. People expect that orchestra seats will cost more than balcony seats, that hardcover versions of books (or books containing many color prints or maps) will cost more than paperbacks, that Tuesday afternoon is a less convenient or enjoyable time to go to the cinema than Friday night, that items available now are more valuable than ones that will not be available for a number of months, or that a concerto performed by the local orchestra but with a world-renowned guest soloist will be a bigger draw than with a local, unknown soloist, and will in turn understand the price differences, and can make choices about whether to buy the high-quality or lower quality option.

Likewise, customers understand the difference in value between a package shipped overnight and one that will take two or more days, or between a standard and luxury model of an automobile, or between premium and regular gasoline. The university where I teach has different prices for football games according to the prestige of the opponent. But anyone going to a football game knows which visiting teams are traditionally very strong and which visiting teams are from a lower division. The athletics department is not revealing an inside secret by pricing different games at different rates.

Where price differentials cannot work is when the seller is revealing something about the quality of the art that would otherwise be unknown to the buyer.

Finally, notice that sellers offering lower quality, lower priced options works to the benefit of consumers, even when the lower quality has been deliberately manufactured by the seller. On the surface it might seem ridiculous that a company would install chips in a printer whose sole purpose is to make the printer work more slowly, or for a theatre to make people queue to purchase tickets on the day of the show when computers and software are all in place to enable purchases to be made online. But these artificially created inconveniences work to enable households to purchase printers for home use when they would otherwise be too expensive, and have enabled many college students on a budget to experience seeing a play on Broadway. I am glad there are paperback books, even if their release is slow, as I am glad there is the option of purchasing slower shipping speeds than guaranteed-overnight.

When pricing quality differentials, arts managers should keep in mind the larger goal of strategic pricing: to obtain from strong market consumers the higher amounts they are willing to pay for your offerings, while offering a discount that weak market consumers, but only they, will use as the inducement to bring them to make a purchase. Manipulation of the quality differential in order to execute this strategy is fair game – it does not lack for transparency – and gives those with less ability to pay a chance to enjoy what you have to offer.

Sources

A seminal theoretical analysis of price discrimination based on quality differentials is Rosen and Rosenfield (1997). That the limits on price discrimination based upon quality can be at least partially solved by adopting the nonprofit organizational form is found in Hansmann (1980; 1981). The case of the slow LaserPrinters is in McAfee (2002). Clerides (2002) looks at price discrimination in the publishing industry. Leslie (2004) provides an empirical study of discounted day-of-show tickets and price discrimination in Broadway theatre. Eckard and Smith (2012) and Courty and Pagliero (2012) in separate studies estimate that the gains from price discrimination based on quality of seats are on the order of 4 to 5 percent in the pop music concert sector.

7
PRICING QUANTITY

It is commonplace for museums to offer single-day tickets or memberships for families that cost less on a per-person basis than would be charged to a single individual, and this is a fairly obvious recognition of the differential between the willingness to pay of a single individual and a set of two parents with children.

In addition, discounts are given on the number of events attended: festivals offer menus of different numbers of performances to attend, where the cost per event decreases as more events are purchased; performing arts organizations offer season tickets; and museums offer memberships which lower the effective price per visit. For individuals, diminishing marginal benefits work on two levels here. Consider an opera season, where there are options for tickets to individual operas as well as season tickets. The more operas one sees in a season, the lower the marginal benefit for attending one more. But that reasoning applies equally to purchases of oranges or shirts. In addition, however, if one were to purchase tickets for the opera on an individual basis, the person would first choose a ticket to their favorite opera of the season. If they were to buy tickets for a second opera during the season, the second ticket would be for an opera that is less-preferred than the first one, and so the reservation price for that ticket will be less.

This chapter and the next cover pricing when customers can be charged for a purchase of single items, à la carte, or as a combination or "bundle" of items, or be offered a choice between these two or more options.

In particular, this chapter will deal with cases where the bundled purchase involves multiple uses, where each use offers something very similar: for example, a discount that applies to the number of performances an individual wishes to attend. It is true that each performance offers something at least slightly different (a different program of pieces to be performed), but for the purposes of thinking about strategic pricing we can imagine this situation as involving varying quantities of the same thing, much as we see for the varying quantities of goods on the shelf at our local grocery store. This chapter will similarly consider discounts for families and other groups. In the following chapter, on tied sales, we will look at pricing bundles of items that are not the same: for example, an offering of two tickets to the theatre together with dinner for two at a local restaurant, or a discounted package of tickets to quite distinct and different museums.

Two-part pricing, the subject of Chapter 5, involves differential pricing on the basis of quantities purchased; one price is charged for "admission" and another for uses of some feature once admission has been gained, say rides at an amusement park, articles in an online magazine, or performances at a festival, where either the admission price or the price per "ride" could conceivably be set at zero. If the admission price is any amount above zero, then the average cost per ride falls with the number of rides purchased, indicating a sort of quantity discount. So why are we returning to the subject? Two-part pricing is a special case, albeit a commonly used practice, of the general problem of pricing different amounts for different quantities. Economists refer to two-part pricing as "linear": each additional ride costs the same amount whether the patron buys two, 12 or 20. But the more general case can be "nonlinear": the marginal price of the third ride can be different from the marginal price attached to the thirteenth, or to the twenty-first.

In common with strategic two-part pricing, and with pricing different levels of quality (see Chapter 6), the goal is to offer a menu of prices to all customers, anticipating that "strong" consumers, those who highly value the performances on offer and are willing to pay highly for them, will choose the option that results in their paying a higher amount, in total, than what will be chosen by "weak" consumers, those who in general have a lower willingness to pay, and must be enticed into making a purchase. As always, we want the price menu to be such that strong consumers do not find the option aimed at weak consumers so attractive that they choose to buy it instead of what was aimed at strong consumers.

In general, it is best for the arts organization to ensure there is a variety of ticket-purchase options, to most effectively capture the surplus from strong and weak consumers. If the presenter offers *only* a subscription to a season's performances, it would lose some potential audience who do not find that worthwhile, but who would attend a single show. If the presenter offers *only* single admissions, it might lose revenue from some patrons who would be willing to pay for additional shows but only at a rate that allowed for a lower average ticket price when multiple tickets are purchased.

For example, let's imagine strong consumer Samantha and weak consumer William. Suppose Samantha's willingness to pay for individual tickets to the opera this year is as follows: she would pay $50 for one performance of her favorite opera, she would pay $40 for her next favorite (given that she plans on also attending her very favorite), $10 for her third favorite (given that she plans on also attending her first two choices), and $5 for her fourth. Her willingness to pay for a subscription that included tickets to all four operas is then $105. But there does not exist a single ticket price per show that would induce her to spend $105 in total; at any price above $50 per performance Samantha would not purchase any tickets, at a price between $40 and $50 she would buy only one ticket, at a price between $10 and $40 she would buy only two tickets. If the marginal cost to the presenter for seating a member of the audience is zero, offering a season's subscription at $105 is the best way to maximize profits from a customer like Samantha.

Now suppose weak customer William has the following preferences: he would pay $60 to see his favorite opera, but nothing at all for any of the others. If all that was offered by the presenter was a season's pass at $105, then no revenue would be gained from William at all. But single tickets, so long as they are priced below $60, will bring him out to that single show.

Now, of course, the potential audience contains customers with a variety of preferences in terms of their favorite operas, how much they would pay at most for a second opera in the same season, and so on. But this simple example of Samantha and William illustrates the principle that it is best to offer a menu of options, a menu that can gain revenues from both strong and weak customers. Remember that the essence of strategic pricing is to recognize that customers differ in their preferences and willingness to pay for different options, including single-ticket prices and bundles of tickets, and to offer a selection of prices such that the seller can best capture revenues from different sorts of customers. With a menu of quantity options, customers sort themselves into different patterns – economists call this "self-selection" – just as they did with two-part pricing (Chapter 5) and varieties of quality (Chapter 6).

By how much should prices vary for different quantities of tickets? Before answering, it is useful to think about how pricing for various *quantities* of tickets is similar to pricing for various *qualities* of tickets. For example, suppose the presenter is selling single tickets in the balcony of the performance venue for $25. On the one hand, the presenter might offer a better quality of seat for that one performance for $35. On the other, the presenter might offer to the buyer of the balcony seat a ticket to an additional show, at a total cost for the two tickets of $35. In each case, the minimum purchase costs $25, and something "extra" can be added to the minimum at an additional price of $10.

Remember the strategy for pricing options of different quality (see Chapter 6): price the lower quality offering, aimed at weak consumers for this genre of exhibition, at the level such that marginal revenues from that category of ticket equal marginal costs (as explained in Chapter 3), and price the higher quality offering, aimed at strong consumers, at a level that maximizes net revenue from them, with the constraint that the price cannot be so high relative to the differences in the quality of the tickets that the strong consumers start purchasing the low-quality offering instead. The price of the high-quality ticket cannot be taken in isolation, but must be considered in light of what is being targeted at weak consumers, and this places a limit on how high the price of the high-quality ticket can go.

I give this reminder from the previous chapter because it turns out that pricing *quantity* differentials works on the same principle.

I will illustrate this through an example. Imagine a dance company that is going to have a season of five shows. Weak consumers are defined as those who are not regular patrons of the dance, are not willing to spend much on a ticket, but who might attend a show if the price is reasonable to them. Strong consumers are fans of attending the dance, who might be induced to purchase a subscription to all five shows. Strong consumers will still have preferences for one performance over another (whether due to what is on the program, or the time of year), and will have diminishing marginal returns; the more shows they attend, the less value they place upon one additional night at the dance.

The price for a ticket to a single show should reflect, for that market, the price where marginal revenues fall to the level of marginal costs, which, as with most performances and exhibitions in the arts, are very close to zero. Recall, marginal revenue is the additional revenue that is obtained when the price is slightly lowered in order to sell more tickets. If the cost of seating extra patrons is essentially zero, and marginal revenue at the current price is positive (i.e., total revenues would rise if the price were lowered and more tickets sold) then the organization is not pricing optimally. In that circumstance it should lower the price, sell more tickets, and gather the extra revenue. When price finally reaches a level such that marginal revenue becomes zero, so that lowering price any further would bring no additional revenue, then the seller has the optimal price.

The price for a subscription will be less than the price of five individually purchased tickets, and will be set at the level that maximizes revenues from the strong consumer base that buys the subscriptions, tempered by the fact that the dance company does not want to price subscriptions so high that strong consumers simply opt for buying one or a few (but not five) individual tickets.

If there were a clear and simple formula that arts organizations could apply to pricing subscriptions it would be given here, but, unfortunately, there is not. Even the most sophisticated economic analysis of this difficult problem remains at a very high level of generality. Arts managers must work within a framework that provides guidelines, as I have tried to give here, but there are no quick and easy solutions to the pricing of quantities.

That said, when it comes to pricing differentials in terms of quantity, or quality, there are some rules of thumb that can be strategically applied. As introduced in Chapter 2, we know that strategic thinking involves looking at the expected effects of changes at the margin. Consider these two examples.

In the first, imagine a theatre company, with a season of four shows. Suppose that in the previous year single tickets were priced at $18, and a subscription package with tickets to each of the four shows was available for $52. Imagine, as we usually do, that the cost of giving the customer a ticket entails no marginal cost to the company. When prices are to be set for the forthcoming season, the manager would first consider the single ticket price of $18. It should be the case that either lowering or raising the single ticket price by a small amount, holding the price of subscriptions constant at $52, would yield no additional aggregate revenue. It will be important to look at combined revenue from individual tickets and subscriptions, with this change in single ticket price. For example, suppose we look at lowering the price of single tickets from $18 to $17. This will increase demand for single tickets from those who were previously not attending any shows at all (whose reservation price for a first ticket was something between $18 and $17), and will increase demand by those who might have previously been willing to purchase one, or two, individual tickets but who might now purchase three. We lose revenue in two ways. First, those who were buying individual tickets, and do not change the quantity purchased, now pay less per ticket than before. Second, some revenue might be lost from those who would have other- wise bought a subscription at $52, but who find with the lowered price for individual tickets it is no longer worth buying a subscription. For example, suppose Jenny is really only interested in seeing three shows, but places no value on the fourth. At an individual ticket price of $18, she found it worthwhile to purchase a subscription at $52, which is lower than $54, the price of three individual tickets at $18 each. But if individual tickets are only $17, she is better off just spending $51 to obtain three individual tickets than she is buying the subscription at $52. Although demand for individual tickets is rising, subscriptions may fall, and less money is being earned from strong customers like Jenny than before.

Now let us turn to the subscription price of $52, and suppose we think about lowering it to $50, holding the price of individual tickets constant at $18. Those already buying subscriptions will now pay less for them, lowering revenues. New subscriptions will arise from some who might have previously bought single tickets, but who now find the subscription a better option; if they previously would have purchased one or two single tickets at $18 each, then revenues from those individuals rise, and if they previously would have purchased three individual tickets at $18, revenues from them fall (why would they ever have purchased three individual tickets, for a total cost of $54, when subscriptions were available at $52? They might have been careless in their spending, simply not "doing the math," or they might have preferred the flexibility of individual tickets, since at the beginning of the season they were unsure how often they could attend). Also, new subscriptions might arise from people who previously bought no tickets at all, of any kind. Suppose Benjamin is willing to pay, at most, $17 for each of three individual performances, but nothing at all for the fourth. At single ticket prices of $18, and a subscription price of $52, he would buy nothing. But he *would* buy a subscription for $50, since that enables him to see three shows he values at $51.

The examples in the previous two paragraphs, of Jenny and Benjamin, might seem highly stylized: are there really people who are going to change their buying behavior on the basis of a change of a dollar or two in price? Yes. It is true for *most* buyers of any good or service that their purchases do not alter with small changes in price. But there are always some buyers who are very close to a "tipping point," where a small change in price is just enough to cause them to change their purchase preferences. If my local grocery increases the price of a package of cherry tomatoes by ten cents, it is true that the majority of people who went shopping intending to purchase a package of cherry tomatoes will still do so. But there will be at least a few who would have bought at the original price, but on seeing the higher price decide to allocate their grocery budget differently. Total demand for any product is never completely insensitive to price, there is always at least some elasticity in demand.

To summarize this example, if we consider lowering either the price of single tickets or the price of subscriptions, the effects include: (1) bringing in new customers, (2) gathering less revenue from existing customers who continue to purchase the same package, and (3) switching by some existing customers from one offering to another. All of these effects on net revenues need to be accounted for. It will be impossible to predict with perfect accuracy the magnitude of any of these effects – even with constant prices there will be unforeseen, and sometimes inexplicable, changes in consumer buying behavior – but over time, and after observing the history of changing demands in response to changing ticket prices, the strategic arts manager can gain at least some sense of the likely effects of price changes.

Next, consider an art museum, which offers tickets for a single admission and for an annual membership, which provides unlimited visits at no charge. The membership option appears to be an application of two-part pricing, with an admission fee for the year, and unlimited "rides" (to use the amusement park example from Chapter 5). But it is not quite the same, as in this case the membership is not the only option – visitors can also just purchase a one-day pass.

In key ways the museum's pricing problem is the same as that for a performing arts organization: if the single-admission ticket is priced to maximize net revenues from weak consumers, how should the membership be priced in order to maximize net revenues from strong consumers, bearing in mind that the higher the membership fee, the more strong consumers will opt for just buying single-admission tickets?

This will vary across different museums; a key variable will be the expected number of visits by strong customers. If the institution is large enough, or has sufficiently varied programming, that even after multiple visits there is still something new for the visitor to enjoy (along with old favorites), then more annual visits would be expected, and the membership price can be correspondingly higher. If the location of the museum is such that there are significant travel costs for most visitors, then we would expect even strong customers to make fewer annual visits although making the most of what visits there are.

Why offer memberships at all? There might be reasons beyond the basics of strategic pricing of admission. For example, memberships can be seen as a means for nonprofit institutions to cultivate donors (we will discuss special issues in pricing for nonprofit organizations in Chapter 10), or to build a database of visitors that can be used in marketing, or as a means of creating stability in revenues, as members will often renew annually even though their initial enthusiasm for the institution might wane somewhat over time. Still, there is actually a pure pricing motive that arises in selling memberships that include unlimited visits, as opposed to, say, restricting the price menu to single admissions, plus some options for discounts on buying a pass that gives some fixed number of visits at a discount off the single ticket price.

To see this, imagine a museum that did *not* offer memberships, but that sold single admissions, and books of five and ten daily admissions, where the books of tickets have a lower per-visit price than the single admission. It could be that a single admission is $13, a book of five visits can be purchased for $50, and a book of ten visits is available for $75. Anybody who knew they would visit between four and six times should buy a book of five tickets, and anybody planning on visiting seven or more times should buy a book of ten tickets. Suppose the marginal cost to letting an additional visitor through the turnstiles is zero. Should the museum introduce an annual membership with unlimited visits? Yes.

To see why the membership is a good idea, let's imagine Sekou is a *very* strong patron of the museum. Suppose he happily buys one book of ten visits for $75, and plans on actually using all the tickets, letting none go to waste. But it is also the case that, even after ten visits, Sekou still would be interested in visiting the museum on more days. However, given diminishing marginal returns, the most he would pay for an eleventh visit is $5, the most he would pay for the twelfth visit is $3, and the most he would pay for a thirteenth visit is $1. In this circumstance, Sekou will buy a book of ten tickets for $75, and that is all; the price is too high for him to buy any additional visits. But he would pay at least $84 for a membership: the $75 (or more) he was willing to pay for the book of ten tickets, plus the $9 ($5 + $3 + $1) he is willing to pay to have an eleventh, twelfth, and thirteenth visit. Since allowing Sekou the extra visits costs the museum nothing, it is smart to offer a membership that gives him those extra visits, and gain more revenues from him.

Although I have illustrated with a specific, stylized example, it is actually a very general result from the economic analysis of pricing: if the seller is going to offer a variety of "quantity" options, it always makes sense to have a highest quantity option where the buyer effectively pays a price per additional unit equal to the marginal cost to the seller. If marginal cost is zero (as it would be in uncrowded facilities), then there ought to be on the menu an option – it will carry the highest price – that allows for unlimited quantity. This finding is related to something we found in the setting of two-part prices in Chapter 5: if at the margin the buyer would value a few extra units (rides at the amusement park, visits to the museum) at an amount higher than it would cost the seller to provide them, then those few extra units should be priced at marginal cost, and this allows the seller to charge more for overall access (admittance to the amusement park, a membership to the museum).

In the final topic of this chapter, let us look at discounts for families and other groups.

A per-ticket discount given to a family of four for a single day admission to a museum, botanical garden, or zoo, is different from a per-ticket discount given to a person who buys a book of four, single-admission tickets to be used on different days. The family discount is more akin to market segmentation (see Chapter 4), where the reservation prices of someone making a purchase on behalf of a household are lower, on a per-person basis, than the reservation prices of a single individual. This is made evident by the fact that we tend not to see discounts given to, say, a group of four friends who all wish to attend the museum at the same time.

To recall the findings of pricing through market segmentation: the optimal strategy is to treat "individuals" and "families" as if they are separate markets, and for each market segment the seller will want to gain an estimate of the demand curve (the expected demand for tickets across a range of potential prices), and then in each market segment to find the price where the marginal revenue (the additional revenue gained from lowering the price slightly in order to sell a few more tickets) is equal to marginal cost (the cost to the seller of allowing a few more people into the facility). The demand curves for individuals and families will differ according to the preferences of each group, and the cultural and recreational opportunities that lie elsewhere, and at what prices. The differential prices can be applied to both single-day admissions and to memberships, and can be tailored to various segments; for example, the local zoo in my nearest big city offers various discounts on memberships for (1) parents and their children; (2) parents and their children and two guests; (3) parents, grandparents, and children; and (4) parents, grandparents, children, and two guests.

Discounts for larger, non-family groups are often offered, and again this is an example of market segmentation. A group of people on an organized, planned visit to a city will have a different reservation price, per person, than an unorganized, unrelated random collection of tourists. In addition, the organized group will also possess some bargaining power; the possibility of selling a bundle of 50 admissions to the museum is attractive to the museum manager, and the tour operator will have an opportunity to try to negotiate a lower price for the group. Across the economy it is common for large-scale buyers to use their market power to negotiate lower prices from sellers; it is less common in the performing arts or museum world, since sales are generally to individuals and, sometimes, families, rather than to large corporate buyers. But group tours, and school districts, are an exception.

The results of bargaining over price between a seller and a large-scale buyer are difficult to predict. But there are a few factors that provide the seller with some strength in such situations. One is that the more unique is the offering of the seller, the more bargaining power it will have. A world-class museum of art in a city, well-known to visitors with cultural interests, will be able to maintain a higher priced group rate, even in the face of bargaining, than a smaller museum that is one of many, where the buyer has greater ability to say "Your price is too high, we will simply visit other attractions instead." A second source of bargaining power for the seller is to attempt to remove the possibility of negotiation, but to post prices for groups that are "firm." That enables the seller to tell the buyer, who might try to negotiate a lower price, "I cannot give you a deal, because I would be in too much trouble with other buyers who have paid the posted price. If I negotiate with you, I would need to do the same for everyone." Tying one's own hands can often prove to be a source of strength in bargaining.

Sources

The (theoretically challenging) economics of nonlinear pricing is covered in Chapter 4 of Shy (2008). Varian (1989) shows the similarity in pricing different levels of quality and quantity. McAfee (2002) gives a nice explanation of the rule that sellers should offer to their strongest buyers an option where marginal increases in the quantity contained in the package increase the price of the package by marginal cost, but no more.

A classic, non-technical essay on bargaining power between buyers and sellers, worth reading for all arts managers, is Michael Porter (1979). That bargaining strength can come from restricting one's own ability to negotiate is found in the seminal work by Thomas Schelling (1960).

8

TIED SALES

If I search on the internet for tickets to the theatre in London's West End, I will come across packages that offer theatre tickets, dinner for two at a good, but not excellent, restaurant, and perhaps a sight-seeing bus tour, where the total price of the package is significantly less than if I were to buy all of those items separately. But if the goal is to make an attractive offer to potential theatre-goers, why does the theatre company not simply lower the price of the theatre tickets alone? Why offer this package? Similarly, why will airline companies offer vacation packages that include airfare together with a hotel stay?

As with price discrimination through two-part pricing (Chapter 5), varying levels of quality (Chapter 6), and varying levels of quantity (Chapter 7), the key to pricing "tied sales" – combinations of dissimilar goods – is to induce "strong" and "weak" markets for the product to self-select options, where a lower priced and a higher priced option are made available to all potential consumers, but weak consumers opt for the lower priced option and strong consumers opt for the higher priced option. Strategic pricing in these cases involves offering a choice to consumers, but where we expect that different types of consumer will choose differently, to the ultimate benefit of the seller.

With tied sales, the bundle is targeted at weak consumers, where it is expected that strong consumers will forgo the bundle and simply purchase a single item.

Consider the example of a bundle consisting of theatre tickets, dinner, and a sight-seeing tour. The target is the consumer who is part of the weak side of the market for theatre tickets. Imagine a pair of price-conscious tourists to a large city, with many attractions before them but only a limited amount of time. They have some interest in the theatre, but it is not a critical aspect of their visit, and they find the full-price standalone theatre ticket rather expensive for their tastes and budget. But they will need to eat, and might welcome the direction to a good (but not extremely highly priced) restaurant, and a sight-seeing tour. The bundle is attractive enough to get them to purchase theatre tickets that they would otherwise not have purchased. On the other hand, there is a strong market of theatre patrons who reside in the city, who will have much less interest in the bundle; they already know the restaurant scene and have their favorite places, and have no interest whatsoever in a bus tour. The strong side of the market will forgo the offer of a bundle of attractions, and just buy the theatre tickets alone.

Following this reasoning we can see why airlines partner with hotels for "vacation packages." These packages are aimed at the budget-conscious tourist, and are designed such that it is not likely that strong customers in terms of travel will choose the package: the number of days and nights is strictly limited, and the hotels tend to be good but not at the top of the class. Strong customers will choose their own hotel, even at a higher cost, valuing the freedom of choice. Weak customers will be attracted by the low cost of the package. The airline is not simply trying to cut its fares (which would apply to *all* buyers), nor is it simply trying to provide recommendations on hotels; it is offering a package meant to charge effectively different airfares to different customers according to their willingness to pay. Tied sales are a means of price discrimination.

Seen in this light, we can understand that the bundle need not contain products that are related at all; the main point is to offer a discount on some bundled item that the weak side of the market will find attractive but that the strong side of the market will ignore. A former teacher of mine, Preston McAfee (2002), recalls the Detroit men's clothier who offered a promotion "buy a suit, get a drill"; the key thing to look for in that case is which potential suit-buyers would have an interest in a discount on a power drill.

Offering a tied sale brings the arts organization into either partnering with other organizations (restaurants, tour operators, or other businesses), or providing the tied goods "in house." It is worth taking some time to consider this decision in detail.

To begin, recall from Chapter 5, on two-part pricing, the explanation of why cinema owners charge such high prices at their concession stands. They are using the different behavior of strong and weak consumers when attending the cinema to price discriminate: since strong consumers of cinema visits tend to be the patrons most likely to make purchases at the concession stand, it makes sense for the cinema owner to keep ticket prices reasonably low (in order to attract weak customers to attend the cinema) and to gain revenue from strong consumers with a high willingness to pay at the concession stand. But notice that for this strategy to work, the admission prices and the concession prices need to be coordinated. The cinema owner can do this, because she is at the same time the concession stand owner. Her goal is to maximize the *total* profits arising from the two sources of revenue that she owns, not just to maximize the revenues from one source or the other.

But suppose it were the case that the movie screenings and the concession stand had two separate owners, who did not coordinate their prices. In that case, the movie owner would be likely to charge a higher admission than he would if he owned both the movie showings and the concessions together; lower ticket prices will bring more business to the concession stand, but someone whose only source of revenue is the movie box office will not care about that. With higher ticket prices, the willingness to pay for concessions will fall, and that will drive the concession owner to drop the prices of popcorn and candy. The combined profit of the two businesses will fall, since the chance to benefit from strategic pricing has been lost.

Now let us suppose that some price coordination between the two, distinct business owners is possible. The movie screenings owner might say to the concession owner, "We can earn more jointly if I lower admission fees, which will enable you to increase concession prices. Your profits would rise, and mine would fall, but your gain would exceed my loss. If you agree to pay me a portion of your gain, we should be able to find an amount such that each of us has, at the end of the day, higher profits than if we priced in an uncoordinated way." While such an arrangement is possible in the abstract, we can easily imagine the practical difficulties. Each side in the negotiation has an incentive to misrepresent what the bargain is worth to them; the ticket seller will want to overstate how much he would lose from lowering ticket prices, the concession owner will want to understate how much she gains from the opportunity to raise prices. For how long does the price agreement last, and what happens if the spending behavior of patrons changes, or turns out to be very different than first anticipated? How costly is the time and effort that will be expended by both sides in negotiating, and subsequently monitoring, the agreement? These issues, none of them trivial, are avoided when a single owner manages the cinema's tickets and concessions.

But, that being said, there are also costs that arise from having one owner instead of two. The joint owner of the business that exhibits films and runs a concession stand must manage two quite different sorts of enterprises, and have at least some ability in each of them, without being so distracted by one part of the business that the other begins to suffer. While there might be some economies to be made in running multiple enterprises simultaneously – for example, perhaps one employee can handle payroll and employment matters for all aspects of the jointly run business – there are also costs in spreading management thinly across multiple activities that need to be borne in mind.

So having one owner rather than two brings benefits and costs, and the benefits of being more easily able to use strategic pricing across different products are only a part of the larger decision. The optimal arrangement will vary with circumstances. A small performing arts center might find it relatively straightforward to manage its own concessions (and to accordingly take advantage of opportunities for strategic pricing between admissions and concession prices), or it might be complex enough that it contracts with an independent firm to run the concessions within the center. Either option comes with its costs and benefits: the costs of diverting management's attention to the running of the concessions, or the costs of having to negotiate and manage the contract with an outside supplier.

Let us consider the issue of strategic pricing across organizations through another example. Imagine an art museum, one that has a store within the museum, but which has not had the room within its building for a café. There is a café, which has been independently owned, next door to the museum. The owner of the café is looking to retire, and has put the café up for sale. Should the museum consider purchasing the café?

At first blush, in attempting to answer this question, one could ask "Has the café been profitable for the previous owner?" If so, perhaps it could turn a profit for the museum should it take ownership, and that could provide useful, unrestricted revenues to the museum. But, in fact, asking whether the café turned a profit for the previous owner is not the key question; instead, we need to ask about the profits that the *museum* could earn if it were to take ownership. In measuring potential profit to the museum, the key variables are the net revenues that the café would generate under museum ownership, measured against the costs of financing the purchase. It is critical to realize that the prices that other potential owners of the café would be willing to pay for it reflect their anticipated flow of profits; the more income any entrepreneur thinks he can generate from the café, the more he will be willing to pay to take ownership. If the museum were to end up as the highest bidder, and thus the new owner of the café, it can only be because the museum sees the possibility of generating a stream of net revenues from the café greater than any other potential buyer believed they could earn.

Under what circumstances might it be true that the museum is the owner that could generate the highest net revenues from the café? It might be that an association with the museum boosts the café's revenues; customers might enjoy the ambiance of a café that is now a part of the museum. It also might be that the museum can look for innovative ways to cross-market its café and its collection, using each to aid in the promotion of the other. And strategic pricing might be a possibility. If it were found that coffee is a draw for the weak side of the market for people visiting the museum, then admission to the museum might be offered with a free cup of coffee at the café afterwards (keeping in mind that the marginal cost of serving a cup of coffee is fairly low relative to the price typically charged).

So there are certainly possibilities for the museum in owning the café in terms of marketing and pricing. But it must be remembered that these gains need to outweigh the costs of expanding into new areas of expertise for management.

Sources

The case of "buy a suit, get a drill" is from McAfee (2002). Two classics on the optimal "scope" of the firm – the activities that could profitably be handled within the firm, opposed to those activities that are best carried out by other firms with whom one could form business relationships and contracts – are Ronald Coase (1937) and Oliver Williamson (1975). A more theoretical treatment is given in Chapter 1 of Tirole (1988).

9

DYNAMIC PRICING

Dynamic pricing is the practice of having the price of a particular event – say a concert to take place on the evening of June 16 – varying over the weeks for which tickets are available for purchase. There are two ways in which prices may vary over time. One is where the information is made public, well in advance, that prices will change in a very specific way. For example, it might be announced that tickets are to be initially priced at $12, but will cost $15 if purchased on the day of the event. The other is where the seller announces in advance that the ticket price might (or might not) be changed over time in response to demand, with prices rising should demand be unexpectedly strong and falling if unexpectedly weak. This variant of dynamic pricing is also known as "yield management," and is familiar to us as a practice in the airline and hotel sectors, but has only recently begun to take hold in the arts and in sports. In this chapter we deal with these two methods of dynamic pricing in turn.

Why set ticket prices for the June 16 concert at $12 for advance purchases but $15 on the day of the show? There are two things going on at once: buyers are being given an incentive to buy early; and a higher price is collected from those buyers who did not respond to the incentive, but did purchase on the day of the show.

There are multiple reasons to incentivize an early purchase. One is that those who buy early effectively become a part of the presenter's marketing team, telling others that they have bought tickets and perhaps encouraging others, directly or indirectly, to join them. The early ticket buyers create a "buzz" in their community for the concert, and this can generate additional sales.

A second reason to incentivize early purchase is that it generates useful information regarding demand for tickets. If demand for tickets is unexpectedly strong, it may be that the number of staff and volunteers on duty the night of the performance will need to be increased. It might also be information that is useful in deciding whether the concert ought to be moved to a larger venue, or if there should be an additional performance. If buyers have no incentive to buy early, then it might only be on the day of the show that it is discovered that the venue is too small, or that there was enough demand for a second concert.

Third, incentivizing early ticket purchase reduces demands on your staff on the day of the show, when they will have other duties arising from the event itself – dealing with any problems that may have arisen for members of the audience, for example. Having most tickets sold in advance reduces the need to bring in extra staff for the night of the show.

How big should the price differential be between advance and day-of-show purchases? As a thought experiment, consider the marginal benefits of widening the differential between the two prices. The marginal benefits include additional sales that arise from the momentum generated from early sales, the usefulness of the information gathered on the expected level of final demand for the show (which can confirm whether the venue is the appropriate size, and the staff resources needed on the day of the concert), and any additional revenue generated by sales made on the day of the show. All of the benefits are declining the wider the price differential becomes: there are diminishing returns to the buzz created by advance sales, the marginal contributions to useful information diminish as increased advance sales take place, and the additional revenue gained from tickets sold on the day of the show will decline, and perhaps even become negative, as fewer tickets are sold on that day, due to forward-thinking consumers opting to buy early, and last-minute customers finding the day-of-show price simply too high to be worthwhile. When marginal benefits have reached zero and would become negative, the optimal price differential has been achieved.

In addition to the reasons to incentivize early purchase given above, there are also opportunities for indirect price discrimination. The pattern is familiar from the previous chapters: the arrangement to buy in advance at $12 or on the day of the show at $15 is offered to *all* potential customers. The price-sensitive customers – the weak side of the market – will be attracted by the discount achievable by purchasing in advance. Those customers who are less price-sensitive will either not really pay attention to the fact that they can buy at a discount with early purchase, or, they might be fully aware of the discount but not care, perhaps because the three dollars in savings is not worth the time and effort to them of buying in advance (even the best advance ticket-selling software takes some time for the customer to use to make the purchase) rather than just paying at the box office when arriving for the show.

This is not to suggest that anyone who purchases higher priced tickets on the day of the show is irrational. To restate what was said in Chapter 1, the strategies in this book are not about luring potential customers into making unwise or irrational decisions. However, a consumer can be entirely rational and still pay a higher than average price for goods when the consumer does not find it worthwhile to expend energy on the discovery and exercise of lower priced options. The concert-goer who buys a higher priced ticket on the day of the show might have been wary about making a commitment for that evening, might not have found it worth the time to go through the procedures for buying an advanced ticket, or might be too busy to keep up with the local schedule of upcoming events. None of these behaviors are irrational, and as consumers we all occasionally cut corners in our search for best prices and quality of product. As an aside, note how well large grocery stores price discriminate on these grounds. Lower prices are offered to all, but are exploited only by price-conscious consumers, in the form of coupons offering discounts, affinity cards, and random sales on durable goods (which can be stored by the customer for later use). Less price-conscious customers forgo these offers, not finding it worth the time to sort through coupons, or to purchase a dozen cans of chicken noodle soup because the price happens to be unusually low that day. The difference in the two types of consumer is not one of rationality or cleverness, but rather is that the store directs its lower prices to those consumers willing to put the time and effort into finding them.

If there are sound reasons for announcing that ticket prices will be higher on the day of the show, why then do we observe *half-price* day-of-show tickets on Broadway? As described in Chapter 6, this too is a form of indirect price discrimination. But in the Broadway case, it is the price-conscious, "weak" market consumers who endure the inconveniences of purchasing on the day of the show, having to make the purchase in person, and the "strong" market consumers who are willing to pay a premium to guarantee themselves a seat on a specific night, and to be able to make the purchase by telephone or online. It is not a contradiction that community theatre charges more on the day of the show and Broadway offers the chance at half price on the day of the show; in each case the presenter is differentiating between customers according to who is less willing to endure inconveniences in making purchases.

Now let's turn to the other form of dynamic pricing, where the price changes according to revealed demand after tickets have initially gone on sale.

To begin, notice that a seat at an arts event is like a seat on an airline trip or a room for a night in a hotel, in that these are, from the point of view of the seller, completely perishable goods. Imagine a fruit and vegetables stand where every night, overnight, all the produce became spoiled and could not be sold the next day. Or think of a clothing store where every night moths came and ruined every single piece of inventory. Tickets for performances, or for trains and airplanes, or for hotel rooms, are just like that: anything unsold cannot be held as inventory and sold later. If a concert takes place on June 6, unsold seats cannot be held and sold at a later time, any more than can unsold seats on the 9:10 p.m. flight from Seattle to Salt Lake City. If demand for a concert, or hotel rooms, is leaving a lot of excess capacity, then the seller would ideally like to find some way to fill that capacity, if possible, since the marginal costs of taking on additional customers is low (although for a hotel it is not zero, since a room that has been occupied subsequently needs cleaning). We know (see Chapter 3) that sometimes the optimal single ticket price will leave some empty seats, if the change in revenues from charging a lower ticket price in order to fill the hall would be negative. But what if the concert presenter, like the hotel manager, had the option of lowering the price only for the tickets that remain unsold as the concert date approaches? A hotel manager will offer reservations at a lower price when it appears that a lot of rooms are going to remain vacant on a particular night. Should the concert presenter also use dynamic pricing?

But there are important ways that cultural goods are *not* like flights or hotel rooms, or even attendance at sporting events. Specifically, think about how consumers make choices in purchases of art and entertainment. Consumers are faced with a vast array of choices regarding books, recordings, movies, and performances. But buying, and actually enjoying, any of these entertainments takes time, which for everyone, whether monetarily rich or poor, is limited. We can only possibly attend a limited number of performances or films, can only possibly read in a year a very small fraction of the number of books available to us. A key factor that guides consumer choice in the arts is the behavior of other consumers. If a book is on the best-sellers list for a large number of weeks it informs the potential buyer that many other readers have found the book worthwhile, and so at least warrants consideration. If a play in town is selling out most of its performances, it signals to the potential member of the audience that the "word of mouth" for the play must be good, even if that individual has not spoken personally with someone who has seen the play. The fact that demand for tickets is strong suggests that some people must have heard good things about the play, and are responding by purchasing tickets. And, conversely, if ticket sales for the show are weak, and are revealed to be weak, it suggests to those who have not yet seen the play that the quality of performance is lacking, that it is not generating positive recommendations. It remains an open question as to whether the creative goods that end up as best-sellers are, by some critical measure, the highest *quality* creative goods. An optimist might say that it is only a creative work with some positive value that can garner that initial spark of sales, especially to influential buyers, that launches a cascade of purchases by the wider market, and a pessimist might argue that there is a large degree of luck involved in which creative goods get early sales, which in turn generate even more sales to buyers who uncritically follow whatever everyone else is buying. Whichever case is true, it remains a fact in the arts that strong sales, or weak sales, send an important signal to those who have not yet sampled the product.

Cultural goods are *experience goods* in the way that airline flights are not. Consumers know in advance what a flight from Seattle to Salt Lake City is all about, and if it is revealed that demand for tickets on a specific flight is unexpectedly high or low, it does not influence any particular consumer's feelings about whether that is a flight worth taking. Low demand for a flight would not make anyone change their mind about whether Salt Lake City is all that interesting. But unexpectedly low demand for a cultural good *does* convey something to the potential buyer, that perhaps those who have experienced the good have found it wanting, and that this information has flowed through the marketplace of cultural consumers.

Lowering prices in response to unexpectedly low demand is thus different in the case of cultural goods than in the case of airlines or hotels, because the act of lowering the price serves as a signal to the market about the quality of what is on offer. Seen in this light, even sports events are quite different from cultural goods. Consider a professional hockey team that by mid-season has been revealed to be near the bottom of the league. As a result, ticket sales for the remaining games in the season are weak. Suppose the team begins to lower its prices for the remaining games, hoping to boost sales. In so doing, the team is not revealing anything about the expected quality of games; anybody who follows the sport already knows that the team is having an off year, and lowering ticket prices might be a sound strategy given the weak market. Ticketing for sports events can resemble ticketing for cultural events in many ways; there is market segmentation with discounts for students and seniors, there is two-part pricing when it comes to setting ticket prices relative to concessions (I once attended a major league baseball game, paying $1 for a ticket in the right field bleacher seats, and $9 for a plastic cup filled with watery beer!), and differential prices according to the quality of seat, and the quantity purchased. But it is a mistake to conclude that sports teams adopting the practice of lowering ticket prices when demand for tickets has turned out to be rather slack provides a useful new strategy for arts organizations. The effects on consumer perceptions are quite different between sports and the arts.

Arts presenters must thus be very cautious when prices are lowered in response to demand. Indeed, we could take the implications of the importance of quality signals in the arts even further. Suppose a publisher of literary fiction releases twelve new novels for the fall season. It prices eleven of them, in hard-cover, at $25, but it prices the twelfth at $15. Will the last novel be its biggest seller? There are reasons to expect it might do the worst. Novels take many hours to read, and the cost of those hours for any one book is going to exceed any small difference in the price paid for the book. If the $15 price on the twelfth novel is taken by consumers as some sort of signal from the publisher that it has rather low expectations of well it will be received, then the low price causes lower, not higher, sales. As a consequence, we expect that sellers of a collection of creative goods will be wary about charging varying prices. Publishers will set the same price for all of their novels. Prices might vary according to easily observed characteristics of books; nobody is surprised that an art book with many, large, high-quality reproductions will be more expensive than other books. But if a collection of books, or CDs, is at first glance comprised of fairly similar items, the seller will be reluctant to charge different prices.

Again, this highlights a difference between pricing cultural events and sporting events. The football team at the university where I teach plays a home schedule that includes teams from the top conferences and those from lower divisions. There is a difference in the ticket prices for opponents of different prestige. But that is a workable strategy for the team because almost everyone who attends the games *knows* which teams are from lower divisions, and expects those ticket prices to be lower. The team is not revealing any-thing by charging different prices for different games. But a theatre company that priced some plays higher than others in its season would be sending a message about the expected quality of the performance, and the lower priced plays could face the lowest demand of all.

There are some circumstances where changing ticket prices after their initial release for sale could make sense, but they are situations where, in changing the price, the seller is not sending any signals about quality. For example, suppose a theatre is producing a well-known work over the holiday season, and schedules many evening performances. The theatre announces in advance that there will be dynamic pricing as follows: for evenings where demand is particularly strong prices might increase, and for quieter nights it would decrease. This is a plausible strategy. If the price for the December 16th performance is lowered but the price for the December 17th performance is held constant, nobody will get the impression that the performance on the 16th is somehow of lower quality than the following evening's performance. If the theatre is transparent with its customers about its pricing policy, it will avoid any confusion over why exactly ticket prices are being adjusted.

But even in this simple case the theatre company needs to take care. Consumers are well aware that hotels and airlines adjust individual prices according to demand patterns, and almost everyone knows that on an airplane the people seated around you will have paid different amounts for their tickets, typically according to when they made their purchase. But we don't know exactly what others paid, only that it is likely different from our own fare. This is a method of pricing to which travelers have become accustomed. On the other hand, if ticket prices are adjusted mid-stream for an arts event, it will be clear to patrons whether they paid more, or less, than others. And with varying prices not being very common in the arts, this could generate customer complaint. Although economists believe in the virtues of the price system as a means of allocating scarce goods to those who value them most, the public often takes a very different view, especially when goods they need to, but have yet to, purchase undergo a price increase based upon increased demand. Sellers are accused of exploitation of consumer needs, of "gouging," when raising the price of goods whose demand has suddenly increased, making the good increasingly scarce.

Arts organizations are always interested in potential new means of garnering revenues, and in recent years there has been increased attention devoted to whether there might be strategic opportunities in dynamic pricing. But there are many pitfalls, and for now at least it is unclear as to whether this tool has much to offer arts managers.

Sources

Pascal Courty (2003) has written about the economics of dynamic pricing in the arts and entertainment. Bikhchandani *et al.* (1998) provide a very useful survey of the economics of consumers learning from the behavior of others. Also see Gary Becker (1991) and Richard Caves (2000) on this subject.

10

PRICING FOR MISSION

So far in this book we have looked at strategic pricing with the goal of maximizing the profits from the presentation of the artistic offerings. Yet many, perhaps most, readers of this book work in, or intend to work in, the public or the nonprofit sector. In this chapter we look at occasions when an organization might depart from profit-maximizing pricing strategies in order to further the cultural or social mission of the organization. What took so long to get to this topic?

There are two reasons why I have saved mission-based pricing for the last chapter. The first reason stems from an observation I have made when it comes to writings on nonprofit and public sector pricing: that the analysis tends to focus on how such organizations would *depart* from profit-maximizing pricing, without ever explaining how profit-maximizing pricing actually works. In other words, there is no clear sense of the point of departure. In this book I have tried to provide a guide to strategic pricing such that if the organization does wish to depart from it, it has a good sense of the starting point. The second reason is that it is not clear that a nonprofit or public sector arts organization would always *want* to depart from the strategic pricing techniques we have outlined in the first nine chapters of the book. In fact, you don't have to search hard to find nonprofits and public organizations using direct price discrimination, two-part pricing, quantity discounts and offerings of different quality levels for different prices, as well as dynamic pricing.

Why are there nonprofit arts organizations? A defining feature of nonprofits is that, should they have revenues that exceed costs, the profits must be retained within the organization to be used to further the mission under which it was incorporated. Profits cannot be distributed to management, board members, or owners; in effect, there are no owners. An entrepreneur who founds an arts organization, if she chooses the nonprofit structure, sacrifices the ability to turn profits into personal income. But she gains the ability to raise charitable donations. The tax systems of most countries provide incentives to make donations to eligible nonprofit organizations, but even in the absence of any tax incentives, donors will give to an organization that *must* use the funds internally rather than as profits to be distributed to owners. As Henry Hansmann has pointed out, these donations might be critical for the arts organizations' ability to cover costs. For all the price discrimination techniques we have so far covered in this text, there might be no way through pricing alone to capture the very high willingness to pay of some arts patrons, whose inclination to place such high value on the arts makes it feasible to finance major museums or opera performances.

Nonprofit and public sector arts organizations have complex goals. While a commercial firm has a clear motive of profit (although in the commercial arts it remains true that the creative talent is highly motived by the quality of production), nonprofits and public sector arts organizations can have multiple aspects to their organizational mission. A further aspect of this complexity is that stakeholders of the organization will attempt to exert their influence on what they regard should be the priorities of the firm. For example, the creative talent – musicians, directors, curators – in an arts organization might have a preference for a level of quality of their performances and exhibitions that goes well beyond what would be prudent given the costs of such high-quality production and the need for expenditures in education and outreach programs.

What role do prices play in nonprofit and public arts organizations?

The first consideration is the one with which we opened this book: arts organizations need funds to be able to cover their expenses. In the nonprofit and public sectors there are sources of revenue other than pricing: donations and sponsorships, or grants from the taxpayer-funded public sector. But pricing for services still adds revenue for the organization. Importantly, it diversifies the sources of revenue and in so doing reduces the general level of risk should one of the other sources of funding take an unexpected fall. And keep in mind the fact that pricing is a source of *unrestricted* revenue; it comes with no strings attached. Grants from foundations or from the public sector are often tied to specific projects or mandates. Pricing revenue can be used by the organization to further its mission in the best way it sees fit, without being beholden to a specific external stakeholder.

Second, pricing is a method of *allocating* to consumers what the arts organization presents. If, at a price of zero, demand for entry into the arts venue – a performance or a museum – would exceed capacity, then prices are one way to determine who gets to enter (those willing to pay the price) and who does not (those unwilling to pay the price). There are other methods of allocation, besides pricing, that could be used in such a situation. One is that the managers of the arts organization could hand pick on some basis those who will be given an entrance ticket. Allowing people to come in on a first-come-first-served basis is another method of allocation. Each of these methods of allocation has the following in common. First, those who end up with a ticket are a different group than those who would enter under an allocation generated by pricing. That might very well be a goal of the organization, but whether it is or not, that is the outcome. If it is not an explicit goal of the organization, then management needs to ask why it would choose this method of allocation. Second, allocating by the principle of "first come first served," or by management discretion, does not make attending the art event completely costless for the customer. Specifically, attendees need to take some action to ensure they get a ticket, either by taking the time to queue early enough to be assured of a place, or by making themselves known to management as someone worthy of being allocated entrance. It is a general observation from economic theory that if a valuable and scarce good is being allocated on a basis other than a market-clearing price, people who value the good will be willing to expend resources to gain their share.

The third consideration for why nonprofit and public sector arts organizations would want to use pricing is *fairness*. If I attend a performance by my local chamber orchestra, then who *ought* to pay for the costs of running the orchestra and producing the concert? This is a central question for cultural policy, and one on which reasonable people come to quite different answers. I won't try to suggest a "right" answer to the question, but I will outline what issues are in play. In terms of who ought to pay, let's put charitable contributions to one side (how much people ought to donate to the arts would take us very far afield), and make a simple dichotomy between funding from attendees at the concert who have purchased tickets, and funding from the government.

We can classify the rationales for government funding of the arts into three types. The first is what economists refer to as *market failure*, a situation where the prices that arise out of the interplay between consumers and suppliers does not yield an amount of production of the good that is socially efficient. What is meant by "efficiency" in this case? Look back to Chapter 2, and recall that we pointed out there was something good about an outcome that had prices at the margin equal to marginal cost. The reason was that if we wanted to know what level of output was best for the community we would look to equating marginal costs and marginal benefits, and that if the demand curve reflected marginal benefits to consumers, and the quantity of output was where those marginal benefits equaled the marginal cost of production, then the market would solve the problem of the optimal amount of production for society without the need of any government intervention. But what if the marginal benefits to consumers do *not* reflect the actual marginal benefits to the community as a whole from cultural output? Suppose there are benefits that extend beyond those that accrue to the individual consumers who actually attend the arts events? In that case, true marginal benefits are greater than indicated by the demand curve, and the market, without government intervention, will produce an amount of output below the amount that equates marginal cost of production with the true marginal benefits to all of the community. Economists refer to the effects on those not directly a part of the audience or production of arts as "spillovers," or "externalities." The situation can be remedied to a degree by having the government subsidize the production of cultural output, raising the amount of production.

What are those benefits that accrue to the community beyond those to the attendees at the cultural events? It could be that there are benefits to the community from preserving arts organizations and artistic practices for future generations. I might not be able to attend the ballet very often, but I could benefit from others attending if it helped to sustain the dance company and the tradition of ballet for my children or grandchildren to enjoy in the future, or even for myself to enjoy in the future when I have more time on my hands. It could be that members of the community take special pride in the cultural heritage of their city or region, even if only a minority of the community ever actually attends cultural events. Or it could be thought that a lively artistic scene in the local community will aid in economic development, as people and businesses are attracted to come work and live in the region as a result of the cultural offerings. All of these (not mutually exclusive) effects can be said to justify some public subsidy for the arts. It needs to be said that the evidence of market failures in the arts of significant magnitude remains thin.

The second rationale for some public support is what I will call *communitarian*: the notion that the government has a role in shaping the values held by members of the community. In this case, the state subsidizes attendance at cultural events because it wants to use its spending power to influence attitudes. Maybe there is a particular interest in fostering multiculturalism, or a knowledge and appreciation of (what is hoped to be) a shared culture, or the virtues of being a good citizen. Our first rationale for government support – market failure – took the tastes of the community as a given, but questioned whether the market, without government intervention, would yield an outcome that was efficient from the point of view of the marginal benefits and the marginal costs of artistic output and consumption. But the communitarian argument does not take tastes as given, and instead sees a role for government in actively trying to shape tastes in a particular way. The objections to this rationale for government subsidy of the arts center on whether it is appropriate for the state to make judgments regarding what sort of cultural tastes are to be preferred to others, which might be seen as a form of paternalism. To repeat, the questions concerning state support of the arts could fill a lengthy book, and so here we simply raise possible rationales for government subsidy, and leave the deep discussion it warrants to be dealt with elsewhere.

The third rationale for government subsidy of the arts is *equity*: the arts are an important part of a fulfilling life, and the government has a role in ensuring that cultural opportunities are available to all, regardless of the individual circumstances of economics, class, or place of residence. Taking as given the notion that the state has at least some role to play in making opportunities and outcomes more equal across the population than the natural state of affairs generated by the economy, there could be a rationale for the government to bring the arts to a wider audience. The benefits are not only to offer an enriched cultural experience to those with restricted access, but also to ensure that the general population is equipped with sufficient familiarity with cultural heritage and contemporary art to enable them to converse and socialize on a more equitable basis with those who, with no assistance from the state, would be fluent in cultural knowledge. Today's workplace places a premium on abilities in communication, human interaction, and understanding, and shared cultural experiences enhance those abilities.

In rich countries the state subsidizes many goods, with some subsidies targeted at the poor and some provided more universally to the population: education, health care, and housing, to name a few. If the government cares about equality, why not restrict its policies to those that help equalize the opportunity to earn income, and those that redistribute income to those sections of society where earnings are unconscionably low? Why get involved in subsidizing the arts, when it could instead just transfer income to poorer people who could then decide themselves whether to spend some of it on cultural amenities? It turns out that government involvement in the direct subsidy of goods and services – the arts, for example – might in some way be a more effective use of resources than simply transferring income to poorer people who could then make choices on where to allocate their spending. Consider this example: it makes sense for the state to subsidize or run adult literacy programs, as opposed to redistributing income such that, if a poorer person needed an adult literacy program they would have the cash to pay for it. The reason is that a cash transfer sends money to *all* people below a certain income threshold, when only a small number of them would actually benefit from an adult literacy program. In-kind provision of the literacy program is a better way of targeting benefits to those who most need them. And nobody would falsely claim such a need, because why would anyone want to lie their way into a literacy program when in fact they could already read?

So let us ask: are cultural offerings akin to the adult literacy programs of the previous paragraph? Is it the case that the government would like live performances to be accessible to low-income individuals who would truly enjoy being able to attend the symphony, but that the number of such people is small, and so the best way to ensure equality is not to simply transfer income to the poor, but also to subsidize, through grants to arts providers, and tax benefits to those who donate to the arts, the consumption of the arts by that small number of low-income art lovers? Public subsidy of the arts can be a well-targeted, *cost-effective* benefit to those lower income individuals who would gain the greatest benefits from it. It is true that the effective, aggregate redistribution of income from arts policy will be very small (as has been found to be the case empirically), but that is all that can reasonably be expected given the distribution of preferences for the arts across different income and education levels.

These three rationales for government subsidy of the arts have different implications for the design of the subsidy. Communitarian arguments for state support of the arts will pay more attention to the actual content of the production: does it help to foster the sort of attitudes that the government wants to encourage? Market failure arguments for subsidy will focus upon the artistic production or consumption that has the greatest impact on those not directly taking part as artists or audience. For example, if local economic development is seen as a primary spillover benefit from the arts, then subsidy would be directed at arts production that is most likely to effect development, through attracting tourists, or the in-migration of skilled workers and associated businesses. The equity case for state subsidy of the arts would examine which parts of the cultural world it is most important to make more widely available and accessible, and how best to actually reach the population that is seen as underserved. Public advocacy for the arts can sometimes evade these questions, but they are important. Not everyone believes that the state has a role, any role at all, in subsidizing the arts, and if they are to be convinced that in fact there is a sound case for public subsidy, then there needs to be an articulation of the goals of the policy, and the most effective means of achieving them. Different goals imply different means, and what might be difficult choices in terms of what to fund.

Having said that, let's return to the problem of pricing when there are goals for the organization beyond making a profit. To make the problem concrete, consider a simple example. Suppose the local orchestra finds that a price range, based on quality of seating, for its concert season, is for seats from $25 to $65 for weekend evening performances, if it wishes to maximize profit, based upon the techniques we have covered so far in this book. And suppose also that the orchestra is a nonprofit organization with part of its mission being to bring classical music to a wider audience. Should it reduce its ticket prices?

The benefit from a price reduction is that the size of the audience will increase, and a portion of that increase would be from the population that the orchestra wishes to attract as part of its mission to bring classical music to a wider audience. It would only be a portion, as presumably at least some of the increase in audience is from people already knowledgeable about classical music, but whose reservation price for a ticket is below what was being charged before the price reduction. Importantly, the price cut will reduce the total revenue from the concert, given that by assumption the initial range of $25 to $65 was profit-maximizing (I assume in this case there is no marginal cost to seating an additional member of the audience). If the price cut results in an increase in audience numbers of 10 percent, it follows that 90 percent of the actual audience is paying a price below what they were willing to pay. And therein lies the major problem of trying to reach a larger audience through a blanket reduction in price. For a portion of an arts audience, perhaps a large portion, the price reduction simply means they pay less for a concert which they already had every intention of attending. Furthermore, given the wealth of data indicating that audiences for performing arts and art museums are skewed towards individuals with higher income and higher education levels, the main effect of the price cut might well be a benefit to that segment of the audience that least needs it.

Here is an analogy from the world of tax policy. All rich countries except the United States raise government revenue through value-added taxes (VAT). These are sales taxes applied to all goods and services, where intermediaries receive a full tax credit for any VAT paid on their purchases, so only final consumers end up effectively paying any tax. And the rates are high – in Denmark, for example, the rate is 25 percent. American visitors might be especially surprised to know that the VAT applies to *everything*. The 25 per-cent tax is applied not just to luxuries, but also to purchases of milk, eggs, and bread. How can that possibly be justified, in a country normally perceived as one that places a high value on economic equality? (And Denmark is not the only European country to apply VAT to all purchases.) Don't they care that the poor spend a higher proportion of their income on groceries than the rich do? But the policy of applying the tax to all purchases, even necessities, does have a rationale.

Suppose Mads earns 10,000 Euros per year and spends 1,000 on grocer-ies, while Freja earns 60,000 Euros per year and spends 3,000 on groceries. While it is true that the proportion of income spent on groceries falls as income rises, it is also true that the rich spend more Euros on groceries per person than the poor. This is not a surprising claim; the rich purchase more expensive types of food, and more of it, than the poor. If the government decided to exclude food from the base of the VAT, and the tax rate is 25 percent, the exclusion would save Mads 250 Euros per year, and would save Freja 750 Euros per year. That would be an ill-targeted means of helping Mads. Suppose, instead, the government *kept* the tax on food, and used some of the money raised from Freja and others in her income bracket to make transfers to people like Mads, either in cash payments or in useful public spending, such that he was more than compensated for having to pay tax on food? In tax policy, as in other branches of social welfare, the goal is to have policies that are *well targeted* at the people they are meant to help. It is expensive and inefficient to have policies that aim to help those with low incomes, but in fact give a much bigger benefit to the well off.

Nonprofit arts organizations need to consider this in their pricing poli-cies. Reducing admission prices across the board will *sometimes* be a sound way to achieve the goal of greater accessibility to the arts. But it must be established, in each case, whether a general price-reduction policy is the most effective option, given the desired goal. For it might also be the case that garnering revenue using pricing methods that generate profits will provide the funds that can be *specifically directed* to programs aimed at inclusiveness. Would general cuts in admission rates to the Art Institute of Chicago, or the San Francisco Opera, be the best way to increase accessibility for low-income individuals? Or would that be an expensive policy that works mostly to the benefit of patrons who can afford to pay more, while producing only mar-ginal help to the intended beneficiaries?

To return to our example of the nonprofit orchestra, the issue could be summarized as follows: a reduction in ticket prices below the profit-maximizing level might be a poorly targeted means of bringing classical music to a wider audience, since part of the benefit of the lower prices, perhaps even most of the benefit, will accrue to patrons who would have attended the concerts in any case, and the amount by which any audience increase is actually from the targeted group might be small. This does not mean that the orchestra ought to give up on its mission. But it could suggest that alternative means of achieving its outreach goals should be considered.

Suppose that ticket prices could be set on a scale, as a function of the buyer's income? This is known as a "sliding scale." Such scales are often used for items that loom large in a household budget: rents in a nonprofit or public housing project, for example, or college tuition, where school officials (in the United States, at least) will commonly negotiate discounts on tuition according to the family's financial circumstances. The sliding scale is also used on lower cost items; the American Economic Association, of which I am a member, charges different annual subscription rates according to the (self-reported) income range of the member. Are sliding scales useful in the arts?

In Chapter 4 we discussed market segmentation – charging members of different identifiable groups (students, for example) a different price according to their different demand curves. But this was introduced as a profit-making strategy. If students, for whatever reason, have a lower willingness to pay for tickets to live theatre, then charging different prices to students will increase profits for the seller. As a result, an equity-motivated strategy of charging less to individuals from groups with lower incomes (if that is correlated with lower willingness to pay, as it often will be) looks much the same as a profit-motivated strategy of market segmentation.

Is there more that arts organizations can do? In some countries, discounted tickets are offered to those on various forms of social (income) assistance. This device is not commonly used in the United States, where the political culture is such that for many there is a degree of stigma attached to receiving government aid. In general, there is not much to be gained by trying to target ticket prices more finely to actual levels of income or wealth, as is more commonly done in setting subsidies for housing or school and college tuition, because the stakes are too small. As a buyer, I am willing to reveal private information about my income and wealth when discussing my children's tuition fees and financial aid with their college of choice, in the hope that a more generous package will be offered, but I am not willing to do so in order to lower the price of a theatre ticket by a few dollars. And so, in the arts, sliding scales tend to follow the less invasive method of market segmentation; discounts for students and seniors and, in some of the more progressive nonprofit arts institutions, the unemployed.

In summary, mission-based arts institutions need not depart from the strategic pricing methods that have been discussed throughout this book in order to fulfill aspects of their mission, and in fact a general lowering of prices might be a most ineffective strategy for outreach to non-traditional audiences. Arts organizations can use the revenues gained through ticket sales to accomplish many program-related goals, and arts managers ought to think carefully before voluntarily sacrificing the revenue possibilities that come from setting prices strategically.

Sources

A good source on rationales for public support of the arts is David Throsby (2010). King and Blaug (1976) is a very insightful essay on the necessity for public funding agencies to clarify their goals for arts funding and policy. Henry Hansmann (1980; 1981) (the 1980 reference is less technical than the 1981) suggests that the need for charitable donations is an important explanation of the prevalence of the nonprofit organizational form in the American arts sector. Newhouse (1970), in a model of a hospital but that is ready applicable to arts organizations, explains why nonprofits might be driven to higher quality levels, and their associated higher costs, than is the case in the public interest. Steinberg and Weisbrod (1998) provide a useful, non-technical summary of issues in nonprofit pricing. Netzer (1992) describes how nonprofit arts attendance is primarily from the higher income brackets. Steiner (1997) provides an empirical analysis of a museum's proposal to increase its number of "free days," and Currie and Gahvari (2008) survey the evidence on helping the poor through cash versus in-kind transfers.

BIBLIOGRAPHY

Acquisti, A. and Varian, H.R. (2005) "Conditioning prices on purchase history," *Marketing Science*, 24: 367–81.

Adams, W.J. and Yellen, J.L. (1976) "Commodity bundling and the burden of monopoly," *Quarterly Journal of Economics*, 90: 475–98.

Aguirre, I., Cowen, S. and Vickers, J. (2010) "Monopoly price discrimination and demand curvature," *American Economic Review*, 100: 1601–15.

Barro, R.J. and Romer, P.M. (1987) "Ski-lift pricing, with applications to labor and other markets," *American Economic Review*, 77: 875–90.

Baumol, W.J. (1996) "Children of the performing arts, the economic dilemma: The climbing costs of health care and education," *Journal of Cultural Economics*, 20: 183–206.

Baumol, W.J. and Bowen, W.G. (1965) "On the performing arts: The anatomy of their economic problems," *American Economic Review, Papers and Proceedings*, 55: 495–502.

Becker, G.S. (1991) "A note on restaurant pricing and other examples of social influences on price," *Journal of Political Economy*, 99: 1109–16.

Bikhchandani, S., Hirshleifer, D. and Welch, I. (1998) "Learning from the behavior of others: Conformity, fads, and informational cascades," *Journal of Economic Perspectives*, 12(3): 151–70.

Caves, R. (2000) *Creative Industries: Contracts Between Art and Commerce*, Cambridge, MA: Harvard University Press.

Clerides, S.K. (2002) "Book value: Intertemporal pricing and quality discrimination in the US market for books," *International Journal of Industrial Organization*, 20: 1385–408.

Coase, R. (1937) "The nature of the firm," *Economica*, 4: 386–405.

Courty, P. (2003) "Ticket pricing under demand uncertainty," *Journal of Law and Economics*, 46: 627–52.

Courty, P. and Pagliero, M. (2012) "The impact of price discrimination on revenue: Evidence from the concert industry," *Review of Economics and Statistics*, 94: 359–69.

Cowan, S. (2012) "Third-degree price discrimination and consumer surplus," *Journal of Industrial Economics*, 60: 333–45.

Cowell, B. (2007) "Measuring the impact of free admission," *Cultural Trends*, 16: 203–24.

Cowen, T. (1996) "Why I do not believe in cost disease," *Journal of Cultural Economics*, 20: 207–14.

Currie, J. and Gahvari, F. (2008) "Transfers in cash and in-kind: Theory meets the data," *Journal of Economic Literature*, 46: 333–83.

Eckard, E.W. and Smith, M.A. (2012) "The revenue gains from multi-tier ticket pricing: Evidence from pop music concerts," *Managerial and Decision Economics*, 33: 463–73.

Frey, B.S. and Steiner, L. (2010) "Pay as you go: A new proposal for museum pricing," CESifo Working Paper #3045.

Friedman, M. (1953) *Essays in Positive Economics*, Chicago: University of Chicago Press.

Gil, R. and Hartmann, W.R. (2009) "Empirical analysis of metering price discrimination: Evidence from concession sales at movie theaters," *Marketing Science*, 28: 1046–62.

Goldman, W. (1983) *Adventures in the Screen Trade*, New York: Grand Central.

Hansmann, H. (1980) "The role of nonprofit enterprise," *Yale Law Journal*, 89: 835–901.

Hansmann, H. (1981) "Nonprofit enterprise in the performing arts," *Bell Journal of Economics*, 12: 341–61.

Hazlett, T.W. (2006) "Shedding tiers for a la carte? An economic analysis of cable TV pricing," George Mason University Law and Economics Research Paper 06–05.

King, K. and Blaug, M. (1976) "Does the Arts Council know what it is doing?," in M. Blaug (ed.) *The Economics of the Arts*, London: Martin Robinson.

Kobayashi, B.H. (2005) "Does economics provide a reliable guide to regulating commodity bundling by firms? A survey of the economic literature," *Journal of Competition Law and Economics*, 1: 707–46.

Leslie, P. (2004) "Price discrimination in Broadway theater," *RAND Journal of Economics*, 35: 520–41.

McAfee, R.P. (2002) *Competitive Solutions*, Princeton, NJ: Princeton University Press.

McAfee, R.P., McMillan, J. and Whinston, M.D. (1989) "Multiproduct monopoly, commodity bundling, and correlation of values," *Quarterly Journal of Economics*, 104: 371–83.

Maddison, D. and Foster, T. (2003) "Valuing congestion costs in the British Museum," *Oxford Economic Papers*, 55: 173–90.

Netzer, D. (1992) "Arts and culture," in C.T. Clotfelter (ed.) *Who Benefits from the Nonprofit Sector?* Chicago: University of Chicago Press.

Newhouse, J.P. (1970) "Toward a theory of nonprofit institutions: An economic model of a hospital," *American Economic Review*, 60: 64–74.

Noonan, D.S. (2003) "Contingent valuation and cultural resources: A meta-analytic review of the literature," *Journal of Cultural Economics*, 27: 159–76.

Oi, W.Y. (1971) "A Disneyland dilemma: Two-part tariffs for a Mickey Mouse monopoly," *Quarterly Journal of Economics*, 85: 77–90.

Pigou, A.C. (1920) *The Economics of Welfare*, London: Macmillan.

Porter, M. (1979) "How competitive forces shape strategy," *Harvard Business Review*, 57(2): 137–45.

Robinson, J. (1933) *Economics of Imperfect Competition*, London: Macmillan.

Rosen, S. and Rosenfield, A.M. (1997) "Ticket pricing," *Journal of Law and Economics*, 40: 351–76.

Schelling, T. (1960) *The Strategy of Conflict*, Cambridge, MA: Harvard University Press.

Schmalensee, R. (1981) "Output and welfare implications of monopolistic third-degree price discrimination," *American Economic Review*, 71: 242–7.

Shiller, B. and Waldfogel, J. (2009) "Music for a song: An empirical look at uniform song pricing and its alternatives," NBER Working Paper #15390.

Shy, O. (2008) *How to Price: A Guide to Pricing Techniques and Yield Management*, Cambridge, UK: Cambridge University Press.

Steinberg, R. and Weisbrod, B.A. (1998) "Pricing and rationing by nonprofit organizations with distributional objectives," in B.A.Weisbrod (ed.) *To Profit or Not to Profit: The Commercial Transformation of the Nonprofit Sector*, Cambridge, UK: Cambridge University Press.

Steinberg, R. and Weisbrod, B.A. (2005) "Nonprofits with distributional objectives: Price discrimination and corner solutions," *Journal of Public Economics*, 89: 2205–30.

Steiner, F. (1997) "Optimal pricing of museum admission," *Journal of Cultural Economics*, 21: 307–33.

Stigler, G.J. (1963) "*United States v. Loew's Inc.*: A note on block-booking," *Supreme Court Review*, 152–7.

Throsby, D. (2003) "Determining the value of cultural goods: How much (or how little) does contingent valuation tell us?," *Journal of Cultural Economics*, 27: 275–85.

Throsby, D. (2010) *The Economics of Cultural Policy*, Cambridge, UK: Cambridge University Press.

Tirole, J. (1988) *The Theory of Industrial Organization*, Cambridge, MA: MIT Press.

Varian, H.R. (1980) "A model of sales," *American Economic Review*, 70: 651–9.

Varian, H.R. (1985) "Price discrimination and social welfare," *American Economic Review*, 75: 870–5.

Varian, H.R. (1989) "Price discrimination," in R. Schmalensee and R.D.Willig (eds.) *Handbook of Industrial Organization*, Vol. 1, Amsterdam: North-Holland.

Williamson, O. (1975) *Markets and Hierarchies: Analysis and Antitrust Implications*, New York: Free Press.

INDEX